Pure Emotional Magic

Pure Emotional Magic

The Trick to Vanishing Your Emotional Baggage into Thin Air

Joey Raab

H&T Publishing

Contact information: Email joey@pureemotionalmagic.com or visit us at www.pureemotionalmagic.com.

Cover Designer: Augusto Silva

Editor: Berni Xiong

ISBN 978-1-7332490-1-0

Contents

Dedication

In memory of my beloved father, Norman Raab.

Preface

THE HAIRCUT THAT CHANGED EVERYTHING

Twenty-five years ago, I had a life-changing experience that completely transformed the way I saw the world. On that day, I went to a haircut appointment with a heavy heart because I had just ended a long-term relationship. As soon as I sat down in my hairstylist's chair, he pointed straight to my heart and told me there was a profound sadness surrounding it.

I was completely and totally astounded. How could he have possibly known? I was careful to put on a good show, as if I didn't have a care in the world.

Of course, his observations were right on the money. Beneath my happy veneer was a deep and intense sadness right in the middle of my heart. He assured me everything would be okay—that the sadness would get lighter throughout the day. I chuckled as I thought to myself, *this guy must be out of his mind!*

If I hadn't witnessed it myself, I would never have believed it. By the end of the haircut, it seemed as though I had undergone a magical transformation. I honestly felt as though a heavy weight had been lifted off my chest. I felt much lighter and noticed my breathing had become much deeper. I honestly had no idea what had transpired, but it completely amazed me that I could feel so much happier and lighter in such a short period of time.

THE MAGICAL MOMENT

Weeks after my experience with the hairstylist, I was having difficulty falling asleep one night. Something was weighing heavily on mind, and it affected me emotionally. I sat up in bed and immediately started thinking about "the haircut that changed everything." I wondered if I could make my emotions vanish somehow just as they did on that magical day.

I began praying with great focus and concentration, hoping to lighten the emotions I was carrying. Soon after making the request, I felt a sense of peace come over me as my emotions began to dissipate. Once again, my heart felt light and happy as my breathing deepened. And, once again, I was stunned. In that moment, I realized this important truth:

> *Emotions have no permanence. They are passing energies that can be cleared out. Underneath the heaviness and the baggage that we carry lies incredible lightness and happiness.*

That realization was a defining moment for me that sparked a tremendous passion to learn everything I could about this work.

DISCOVERING THE TECHNIQUE

Can emotions be quickly and "magically" transformed to reveal a lightness and peace underneath?

Is there a reliable way to work with our emotions and release them in every situation?

What about a technique that consistently works magic to help clear out emotions?

Or are these bizarre and isolated incidents that can never be duplicated?

Determined to find the answers, I began a journey to not only uncover what had happened to me, but also to develop a concise technique to help people work with any kind of emotion and release it in a healthy manner.

In doing this work, I have discovered that we do not have to hold onto fear, grief, sadness, anger, or any other emotion. No matter what has transpired in our lives, we have tools and techniques that can free us of the burdens we all carry. And what we find when we release the emotional burden is a lightness and a happiness that many of us have completely forgotten.

Over the years, I've refined this technique by working through real situations in my own life as well as in those of clients and friends. From working through my father's lengthy and life-ending illness to having my home burglarized, these techniques have helped me successfully clear out anger, grief, victimization, fear, and much more. This work has enabled me to process the emotions effectively and let go—returning me to the sunshine.

And while emotions are perfectly normal for us to have, the problem is when we continue to hold onto them indefinitely. This causes the emotions to take up residence and become a permanent part of our experience and identity. After living with grief, anger, fear, and other forms of "stuff," we believe this is how life is supposed to feel! Fortunately, putting down these burdens is the only thing required to return to the natural joy living inside each of us.

Perhaps you haven't had these naturally occurring feelings since childhood, but I can assure you they are still there! You can let the sunshine return...and *THAT* is the purpose of this book.

PURE EMOTIONAL MAGIC

This book is the product of my lifelong passion into self-empowerment and personal growth. It is the fruit of many years of exploring this passion and putting these principles to the test. In this book, you'll receive a step-by-step guide on how to clear out the emotional clutter—what I like to call "stuff"—that is holding you back or keeping you down in life.

If these ideas excite you, I believe this book will be a perfect match for you. Read a few pages and see if the book speaks to you. Books are like songs. Just as songs can profoundly uplift certain people while doing little or nothing for others, books operate similarly. If this book speaks to you, you are about to embark on an incredible journey toward rediscovery—returning to the joy and happiness hiding beneath all the "stuff" you have accumulated throughout life.

No matter what has transpired in your life, you don't have to carry the emotional stuff around with you any longer. You can peel away the layers of emotional turmoil and allow yourself to become much lighter and much happier. *Pure Emotional Magic* will show you how to make your emotional baggage vanish into thin air.

Introduction

Chapter 1 provides important foundational principles for understanding this work before we dive into the specific techniques.

Chapter 2 delves into the actual techniques and methodologies to free you from any past burden holding you back. You will learn the nuts and bolts of this technique.

Chapter 3 goes into more specific details concerning writing the letter or making the request, which is a central part of this work.

Chapter 4 shows you what happens after practicing this work. You will better understand the timetable of how the results will unfold and what to expect after practicing these techniques.

Chapter 5 shares a chronicle of my personal journey into the depths of grief and darkness as I helplessly watched my father slowly deteriorate during the years leading up to his death. Putting the techniques into action, I cleared out the darkness and grief one layer at a time.

Chapter 6 discusses the various types of emotions we all carry with us and addresses each one in greater detail. I also share some of my personal experiences regarding these specific emotions.

Chapter 7 discusses additional information on how this work can help improve our relationships for the better. Though the emphasis is on relationships with our significant others, these principles and techniques can apply to any kind of relationship.

Chapter 8 delves into the more mystical aspects of this work. This chapter is not for everyone, and certainly not a required component of the practice. If you have any interest in the mystical and the esoteric, however, this chapter has your name on it.

Let's get started!

1

The Backpack

Right now, you are carrying a backpack. Not a physical backpack, but an emotional backpack that dramatically impacts how you feel and the way you experience life.

Have you ever tried to look inside your own backpack? What would you find? Is it anger? Perhaps it's sadness. Maybe grief? Possibly guilt? Or fear? As these emotions build up throughout life, they mask the joy that lives inside each of us. For many, it has been years since this joy has surfaced. But this natural happiness is still living inside of you, waiting to be rediscovered.

One of life's greatest secrets is this: *Carrying the backpack is optional.* Only you can decide the reasons for continuing to carry this backpack. Only you can decide "if" and "when" you want to put this backpack down. And that's great news because putting down this backpack will reveal all the happiness and joy that lies hidden inside of you.

You might not be aware of how "heavy" everything feels until you take off this backpack and experience the feeling of being light as a feather. Even your chest will feel lighter as your breathing becomes deeper.

You might not realize all the sadness you carry with you. Taking off this backpack will allow all the happiness to stream back into your awareness.

You might not realize how isolated and numb you feel until you remove this backpack so you can feel connected and alive again.

There are precise steps you can follow to remove this backpack and return to this natural happiness. The results are often so incredible that it seems like pure emotional magic.

Let's take the first step by exploring some exciting key principles.

PRINCIPLE #1 THE FIRST STEP TO FREEDOM

Have you ever seen one of those "head in the hole" boards that people stand behind to take pictures? They are usually wooden boards with a painting of a caricature of a body and a carved-out hole for a head in which to insert your face. You can stand behind the board and instantly appear as the character in the particular destination. Hair, clothing, and location seem to have completely changed from one board to another. Though the scenery changes with each different board, the "real" you stays intact because only the most superficial layer changes. Underneath it all, you are still the same person. Our souls operate in a similar manner, and understanding this premise is the first step to freedom.

Throughout our lives, we will stand behind many "emotional" boards while remaining the same person underneath. Our emotions may come and go, yet our underlying soul and inner happiness remain forever unchanged. These emotions we carry with us act like clouds in front of the sun. The sun continues to shine even when the darkest and heaviest of clouds obscure it from view.

I like to refer to these emotional clouds that hide the light of our being as "stuff." Stuff can obscure all the joy and happiness and hide it beneath the surface.

Anger is stuff. Sadness is stuff. Grief is stuff. What about guilt? You guessed it... more stuff! Since stuff can obscure our true identity—the happiness that lies beneath—the way to happiness and inner joy is nothing more than learning to remove this stuff. In fact, your stuff is the only thing standing between you and the true happiness that lies within. You don't have to haul around your stuff endlessly. You can clear those unwanted emotions out—freeing you from the turmoil and heaviness that can diminish your light.

Your true essence is changeless. Our job is simple: to clear out the clouds and reveal the true and joyous essence that lies beneath. The real you that once stood behind the board will emerge like the sun after the clouds clear. This book will teach you how to live more of your life in the sunshine and how to clear out the emotional clouds when they arise.

Just as clouds are a necessary component of life on earth, our negative emotions are also a vital and necessary part of our total being; there is nothing inherently wrong with these emotions. However, there is no need to dwell in negativity and experience a constant dreary backdrop in our lives.

Even having one experience with clearing out stuff can give you an "aha" moment. Never again will you believe you are incapable of clearing out emotional suffering or returning to a state of happiness. Whether you are suffering from guilt, mired in grief, or riddled with fear, this work can miraculously free you. But don't take my word for it. I want for you to experience the benefits of this book firsthand.

What you are about to read is not only theoretical. The techniques shared within this book are the actual tools I used along my journey. As I learned how to clear out stuff, the more prominently natural happiness surfaced in my life. I knew that if I wanted to experience happiness more often, I'd have to understand the source of this happiness. This book is a practical guide you can use to help you access the joy that has been hiding beneath your stuff all these years. You can learn to peel off the emotions that have been holding you back, one layer at a time, revealing the joy that lives underneath.

PRINCIPLE #2 WHOSE HOUSE IS IT ANYWAY?

Your best friend needs a favor. She lives in a small apartment and is unable to host Scott, a good friend who is coming to town. She would like to know if Scott can stay in your large basement. She assures you it will only be a few days. Reluctantly, you agree to let Scott stay in your large finished basement.

Here's where the story takes a turn for the worse. Scott winds up being loud and obnoxious, staying up all night and having loud parties that keep you awake at all hours. Most evenings you can hear loud music blasting, accompanied by the sound of cars that are constantly coming and going all throughout the night. Cigarette smoke permeates your house, which you find unbearable because of your asthma and allergies.

After a few days, Scott informs you he would like to extend his trip and stay with you for the rest of the week. Since you find it difficult to say no, you begrudgingly consent. You endure yet another week of loud parties accompanied by strong cigarette smoke, waiting for Scott's visit to mercifully come to an end. The days creep by and finally the week ends. At the end of the week, Scott does the unthinkable. He asks if he can stay with you indefinitely as he is considering moving to town and would like to further explore his options. As preposterous as it sounds, you agree to let Scott stay with you indefinitely as he figures out his transition.

One month later, Scott is still living with you! One month turns into two and then three. Six months later, Scott is still wreaking havoc inside your house! At this point, Scott has started bringing his new girlfriend around the house. She is practically living in your home as well. The loud parties continue. The smoking continues. Their obnoxious friends are also hanging out at your house until the wee hours of the morning. You have become totally and completely miserable and are now at your wits end.

To cope with your new environment, you see an allergist regularly who has prescribed numerous allergy medications to help you tolerate the smoke. In addition, you are now spending countless hours and dollars each week for psychotherapy and anti-anxiety pills. And, on some of your worst days, alcohol is your friend when all else fails.

You ask yourself: *How utterly absurd is this situation? Who on earth would let something like this happen?*

We can often see the solution so much easier when a situation is happening to someone else. If your friend were in the same predicament and sought your advice, the answer would be crystal clear: get Scott and his friends out of your house!!! Not tomorrow, not next week. Right now! The reason your house is being overrun by loud and obnoxious guests is because you've forgotten **YOU** are the owner of the house! As the owner, **YOU** get to decide who stays there. And **YOU** get to decide who leaves.

Many of us have found ourselves in a similar situation. We are living in a house overrun by our stuff. We have forgotten who is in charge of the house. We have had the power all along to ask our guests (the stuff) to leave, yet we continue to allow it to destroy our peace and happiness.

We have forgotten the simple truth: *We decide who gets to stay in our house.*

When we become so accustomed to living with these obnoxious house guests, we can fail to realize we've had the power all along to ask them to leave.

We are, therefore, forced to cope with all of this stuff we are lugging around by resorting to a multitude of coping mechanisms—which can often include alcohol, medications, and professional counseling. It would be so much easier to confront the guests and ask them to leave! Surely, it's worth the temporary discomfort of confronting Scott and asking him to leave for the long-term benefit of achieving peace in your home. The same holds true with stuff. Isn't it worth the temporary discomfort of facing your emotional backpack to regain your freedom, joy, and peace of mind?

This book has come into your life to remind you of the power you have to decide which houseguests get to stay in your life and which ones must leave. It doesn't matter if they've been there for days, weeks, months or years. As you move through this book, you'll learn principles to help you get back your freedom and reclaim your power. You'll learn you don't have to continue to host pain, sadness, grief, anger, and fear. These guests can only stay with your consent. Many of us are unaware we even have a choice in the matter. This book assures you that you do.

PRINCIPLE #3 A HUGE SECRET ABOUT THE GUESTS

Remember watching "The Wizard of Oz" as a child? I have such wonderful memories! I can remember the wizard well. He was very impressive with this incredibly loud, booming voice and tons of smoke that bellowed out. To a small child, the wizard was downright terrifying! No wonder Dorothy was afraid to go anywhere near this wizard!!

What's interesting to note is that all Dorothy had to do was have the courage to walk up to the wizard and look behind the small curtain on the side. When she pushed the curtain aside it revealed a small and harmless old man sitting behind it. The only requirement for Dorothy to make all the fear surrounding the wizard disappear in an instant was to approach the wizard with the willingness and courage to look behind the curtain.

Our emotions operate similarly. The stuff we carry with us can look terrifying from a distance. It is, therefore, quite common to spend years paralyzed by the fear of confronting our stuff. But one quick look behind the curtain is all it takes to expose the true nature of the stuff. Like Dorothy, all we need to do is walk right up to it and pull back the curtain. The very act of looking at stuff robs it of the power we've allowed it to have over us. When you are willing to look at your stuff and stop resisting it, it will begin to change—much like a mirage.

A mirage is an optical illusion that appears real from a distance when, in fact, it does not really exist. You have to walk up close to it to reveal its true nature. The same is true of stuff, which dissipates the closer we look at it.

It's also interesting to note that all mirages are equally untrue, regardless of their respective content. No matter how scary a mirage appears, walking up to it reveals its true nature. The same is true with stuff no matter how scary it might seem.

Think of our consciousness as a bright light shining in the dark. When we look directly at our stuff, it is tantamount to shining that flashlight in a dark room, instantly dispelling the darkness.

Shining the light on our stuff will require us to face it and interact with it. As you move through this book, it is crucial to keep this concept in mind since this important principle helps make your stuff seem much more approachable and also lessens the fear surrounding our emotions. Emotions might not always feel good, and that's okay. The peace you will experience after clearing out the stuff will be worth the effort. Releasing it will ultimately bring joyous relief.

Walk up to the stuff with your chin held high. Show it you mean business!

PRINCIPLE #4 THE EASIEST DECISION YOU WILL EVER MAKE

The number one objection I hear to putting down the backpack goes something like this: "I'm not okay with what happened in my life. It's not what I wanted or expected. It's not what I deserved and is completely unfair. Therefore, I'm not willing to let go and put down this emotional backpack."

Maybe you've lost a loved one the way I have. It's not what you wanted. It's not what you deserved. And you're certainly not okay with it. It is completely understandable why you want to continue to carry the grief with you. Maybe your boss fired you or your significant other left you and you're still carrying a lot of anger and sadness because it seemed completely unjustified. It's difficult to put this stuff down, especially when it's not what you wanted or deserved.

Let me ask you a question. Suppose somebody came up to you out of nowhere. You're just minding your business and, for no reason whatsoever, they punch you in the face! We're not talking about a little punch here. They punch you so hard that they break your nose. You're on the ground writhing in excruciating pain!

Would anybody, even for a second, think: *Maybe I won't get my nose fixed because I'm not okay with what happened! I didn't deserve to have my nose punched! This guy had no right to punch me and I'm not okay with it! Therefore, I will live out my days in horrible pain.*

Obviously, that's absurd. Getting your nose fixed has nothing to do with whether you agree or disagree with the person who punched you. You fix your nose to get out of pain! Sure, you would still have to deal with the situation at hand and perhaps even want to sue the guy. But whatever you do, get out of pain.

Why do we treat emotional pain differently? If life metaphorically punches you in the face—say a best friend betrays you or your boss fires you or any other unwanted situation—why not get out of the pain? Even though you are not okay with these unwanted situations, at least get out of pain! Yes, you will still have to deal with these unwanted circumstances, just as the person with the broken nose had to deal with an undesirable situation. But why not heal your "emotionally broken nose" by putting down the backpack and clearing out your stuff?

Just like you would heal a broken nose, it's equally sensible to heal your emotional wounds and get back to the peace. It doesn't mean you're okay with what happened, but it gets you out of pain!

Traumatic life events do not have to become life sentences where we walk around carrying these heavy backpacks.

No matter what has happened to you in life, you can still decide to let go in order to get back to the underlying peace. You will still have to deal with the situation, but you will feel so much lighter, happier, and peaceful once you put down the backpack and return to the sunlight.

PRINCIPLE #5 HAPPINESS'S ONLY REQUIREMENT

Your job is not to *make* yourself happy, but rather to *remove* the obstacles that prevent you from experiencing happiness. And the only obstacle preventing you from experiencing the happiness—your true nature—is the stuff that gets in the way.

Simply put, happiness naturally occurs in the absence of stuff. Our job is to remove and clear out the clouds, automatically revealing our true and joyous nature that lies beneath.

This is a fundamental shift from mainstream thought. People are often trying to obtain happiness while they carry around untold amounts of emotional stuff. This emotional stuff obscures the happiness they are seeking. If they could just put down this stuff, the hidden happiness would naturally come forth.

Rather than focusing on finding happiness, turn your attention towards clearing out the unhappiness. And this so-called unhappiness is nothing more than your stuff.

This book puts an end to the often-elusive search for happiness and asks you to clear out the stuff. As a result, the happiness will naturally and inevitably come forth.

PRINCIPLE #6 HOW CAN CLEARING OUT STUFF MAKE YOU HAPPY WHEN BAD THINGS ARE HAPPENING?

Clearing out the stuff won't change a bad situation, but it will always allow you to achieve peace. Why? Because you are no longer carrying around a mountain of heavy stuff.

Since events that transpire in your life are not the same as the stuff, you can successfully clear out the stuff surrounding a bad situation while you continue to deal with it. It obviously won't change the situation, but it will completely change your experience since you are no longer carrying around all the heaviness, anger, grief, and other forms of stuff that weigh you down and color the way you experience life.

In Chapter 5, I will recount how I lived with the slow death of a parent while clearing out stuff each day. I'm not saying that clearing out stuff made the situation easy. There is nothing easy about losing a loved one, and I miss my father every day. However, I learned how to put down the heavy burden of grief and darkness. Tragic events and the resulting grief and darkness do not have to be forever interlaced. They are separate entities. You can grieve and you can also clear out stuff simultaneously—returning you to the tranquility that lies buried beneath. No, it won't change the situation, but it will dramatically change how you experience your life henceforth.

Tragic events often become life sentences of hauling around heavy burdens throughout our lives. The real tragedy is when we never learn to put the stuff down. The people, events, and issues that stem from the tragedy will still be there—and might not be pretty. But you are no longer harboring all of that darkness and heaviness. You can breathe again. You can feel peaceful again. You can experience the natural inner happiness even amidst all the turmoil because the heaviness and darkness are no longer present.

Each time you clear out the stuff, it will go away for good or return lighter and lighter each time until it completely vanishes. This is how you peel the onion, clearing out layer upon layer of stuff until you are left with nothing but peace. We will discuss this in more detail as this book unfolds. For now, it's important to distinguish between the events in your life you are experiencing versus the stuff you are carrying with you.

We are not talking about shoving the situation or unwanted emotions under the rug. To the contrary, when you confront and clear out the stuff, you are in a much better position to deal with the situation at hand. The principles shared in this book will teach you things you might have never learned: peace is an inside job that lies hidden beneath the burdens we carry.

The goal of the work we will do is to show you how to remove this stuff and rediscover your happy self.

HOW CAN A BACKPACK CAUSE SO MUCH TROUBLE?

Stuff is a real trickster. It loves playing hide-and-seek by disappearing and then springing back into action the next time a person or event triggers it. This explains the crazy phenomenon of road rage. A seemingly normal person will suddenly go crazy and even try to shoot someone simply because they got cut off in traffic. It's possible this person was already harboring a tremendous amount of anger that was never cleared out. The anger went to sleep, waiting for the next opportunity where a person or life event awakens it and brings it back to the surface. Getting cut off in traffic stirred up all of this unhealed anger and brought it back to life.

In many cases, a culmination of yesterday's stuff we've never properly healed drives today's arguments. When stuff gets triggered, it creates a strong and exaggerated response because all the unhealed emotion gets reawakened and propelled to the surface. Other forms of stuff such as fear, sadness, guilt, and anxiety work in the same way. When people or life events stir up our stuff, it's up to us to correctly identify their true source WITHIN, rather than mistaking it for the person or event that only acted as a trigger. If you blame the person or event that triggered your stuff, then the true source within will not be recognized—robbing you of the opportunity to heal and clear out the stuff at its source.

People and events only serve to awaken our stuff within but are often NOT the cause of it. Life can only trigger what is already inside of you. The person or event that makes you angry is usually only triggering an emotion that was already present in a dormant state.

Not only does stuff affect the way you feel, it also colors how you see and experience the world. For example, if you don't heal the anger that was triggered when someone mistreated you, it often continues to smolder in the background of your life—preventing you from experiencing peace. Life is now seen and experienced through a prism of anger which effects the way you think, feel, and perceive.

Anger, grief, sadness, and other forms of stuff are all heavy back-packs that hide your joy and color the way you experience life. They not only weigh us down during the day, but prevent us from sleeping soundly at night. Clearing out the stuff will allow all the hidden joy to once again come out of hiding and return to your awareness. It's the greatest gift you can give yourself!

THE ORIGINS OF STUFF

How on earth was all of this stuff ever created in the first place? What brought it into existence?

There are three sources largely responsible for the creation of stuff. The first two are easy to understand while the last one is more esoteric and elusive in nature.

1) Meet the Mental Narrator. The first way stuff gets generated happens right inside our own head! Many of us are unaware that we live with a heckler inside our mind, which I like to refer to as the mental narrator. For many people, this mental voice engages in constant negative self-talk—spewing out a torrent of negativity day and night—giving rise to a lot of new stuff. It's like having bad music playing on repeat inside our head.

It might say things like:

Why am I so clumsy? I'll never get ahead!

I never do anything right.

Why do we engage in negative self-talk? Negative self-talk is the art of constantly telling yourself negative things. Most of us are on autopilot when we speak to ourselves in a negative manner. Noticing when we do this can help us take control of what we tell ourselves and what we choose to focus on. For many of us, this is the norm to have a negative voice playing in our minds—putting us in a bad mood and creating more stuff.

If you dwell on negative things, you will continue to create more stuff while simultaneously triggering your existing stuff as well. When you ask yourself hypothetical "What if" questions, this can perpetuate the worry and anxiety. Doing this can also trigger any existing worry and anxiety already lying dormant beneath the surface.

Once this stuff gets activated and surfaces, it influences our thoughts and what the mental narrator tells us. For example, sadness or self-pity can influence negative and self-deprecating thoughts, which continue to keep us in a sad frame of mind. And it doesn't stop there. The mental narrator is now charged with a sad state of mind and will begin saying things to create even more sadness. It might tell you about your pathetic life or that you will never get ahead. All of this sad commentary will only lead to the creation of more stuff—thus perpetuating a vicious cycle!

The key is to notice what you are telling yourself and where you are placing your focus. This enables you to catch yourself in the act when you are telling yourself negative things that only serve to create more stuff. Once you are aware of this commentator in your mind, you can step back and recognize what is happening. You can take the voice less seriously and recognize it's just the mental narrator inside your head. You can notice what is happening, yet still take a step back to observe rather than get caught up in what your mental narrator is saying.

To take it a step further, you can even stop this mental heckler by countering with something positive. If the mental narrator says you are a procrastinator, you can catch her in the act and think the opposite: *I get things done in a timely manner.* It sounds very basic and simple, but it can work wonders. Each time you begin thinking about how much you procrastinate, you will catch yourself and reference your new thought: *I get things done in a timely manner.* This can lead to different actions and behavioral patterns and prevent the creation of new stuff.

Imagine if a small child came up to you and called you a loser. Would you take this little child seriously? Would this lead to an existential crisis and put your life in a tailspin? Would you take it to heart and start questioning your self-worth? Most of us would just laugh it off and move on with our day. You don't have to take random comments from young children so seriously. You can let them go and move on.

The same is true for the heckler who lives inside our head. You don't have to take him or her so seriously. Your thoughts are just thoughts. Nothing more, nothing less. You can simply let them go and move on with your life.

An old friend of mine used to have a serious problem avoiding confrontation. Say an intoxicated person were to approach us and become confrontational, most of us would recognize the situation as some drunk guy trying to stir up trouble and we'd keep walking.

Not my friend—he would feel compelled to answer and escalate the situation.

Think of our mental narrator as that drunk guy trying to stir up trouble inside our heads. Just laugh and move on. Otherwise, you can spend years making yourself miserable by dwelling on fearful, sad, or anxiety-producing thoughts. Don't waste your time on these thoughts. Keep walking. The less attention you pay to this mental heckler, the less often he or she will harass you.

It's time to reclaim what is being spoken inside of our heads and turn it into a positive message. This will stop us from creating new stuff and stirring up our old stuff. It gives us the opportunity to change the conversation going on inside our heads and begin focusing on the positive.

2) People and Events. The second way much of our stuff gets generated is through the people, events, and experiences that shape our lives. This starts during childhood, when we are young and susceptible to other people's opinions and ideas about us. Suppose you have a mother who was always critical of you. This could generate all kinds of emotional stuff that stays with you indefinitely and gets activated continually by people and events throughout your life. The only way to break the cycle would be to clear it out once and for all. Major events and life experiences give rise to a tremendous amount of stuff as well. For example, if you suffered loss or tragedy, the grief, anger, and sadness can continue to hang around if it is not addressed and cleared out. It might surface from time to time or become a permanent backdrop for the experiences of your life. And, unfortunately, these patterns will continue to affect our lives until we take the time to clear them out.

Therefore, our past life experiences and the things people have told us are the second major source of stuff that accrues throughout our life.

3) Born with it. The third source of stuff is much more esoteric in nature. Some people are born with a lot of stuff and carry a heavy burden with them right from the start. Perhaps they are carrying it with them from another time and place in a different lifetime. Perhaps this is part of their great task—to transform this inner darkness into light and find their true self hiding beneath the stuff.

Whatever the origins of your stuff, it can always be cleared out. This allows us to find the peace and happiness that's hiding just beneath the surface. And that is the goal of the techniques you will discover later in this book.

IS THERE A "DOWNSIDE" TO REMOVING THE BACKPACK?

Yes. It will be almost impossible to pick it up again! After experiencing life without the heavy backpack, it becomes much more difficult to go back to business as usual. Now that you have tasted the freedom that awaits you, it will be much more difficult to go back. When you have a longstanding discomfort that temporarily stops and then resumes again, the contrast will make you feel even more uncomfortable.

For many people, it's as though the longstanding anesthesia has worn off and they are now much more aware of how painful it is to carry around a backpack full of stuff! This newfound awareness will compel you to no longer carry around your misery mindlessly. You will see your pain in a completely different way as you work with the techniques in this book and let go. Once you experience the relief that comes from letting go, you will never be able to go back to sleep and carry your past hurts with you. The techniques in this book will set you on a course to clear out the stuff and return to the underlying happiness. It will be virtually impossible to go back to being unaware of the burdens you carry. But you will also begin an epic journey to freedom from the past and the reawakening of the real you.

WHAT IF YOU WANT TO KEEP THE BACKPACK?

What if you're not completely sold on this idea, and have no interest in learning the techniques in this book? I believe you picked up this book because you're tired of hauling around this backpack. However, you are welcome to keep the backpack on.

There is nothing intrinsically wrong with holding onto pain. It is your choice to remain as perfectly miserable as you like. Holding onto pain is a choice and, as such, reaps its own reward—namely, living with pain.

It's not a crime to live with pain, but this book is offering you another choice. There is absolutely nothing wrong with choosing the backpack over peace—and nobody can take that right away from you. But if you're tired of hauling around the backpack, this book can provide the means to put it down and live life differently.

In any moment, you can use the techniques shared in this book—allowing you to let go of the stuff you have been carrying around and finally put down the backpack. It's never been a matter of *if* you can let go; rather, are you willing to let go? If so, your life is about to change in ways you could have never imagined.

This is your ticket to letting go of the burdens that have been holding you down so you can walk into the sunshine.

CHAPTER 1 SUMMARY

Emotions, referred to as "stuff" throughout this book, are a normal part of life.

Stuff that is not processed and cleared out can wreak havoc in many different ways—masking our joy and coloring the way we experience life.

Only you can decide the reasons to continue carrying these emotions and when to put them down.

There are techniques that will enable you to clear out these emotions and rediscover this natural joy, including the techniques in this book.

Like the Wizard of Oz, stuff only looks scary before you look behind the curtain and confront these emotions.

Confronting anger, fear, grief, and other forms of stuff is a great first step in the releasing process.

Clearing out stuff won't change a bad situation, but it will completely change your experience by removing the dark and heavy cloud that is weighing you down. Removing the stuff reveals the underlying happiness that lives inside each of us.

Your job is not to make yourself happy, but to clear out the stuff. This will automatically reveal the underlying happiness.

If someone wrongfully punched you in the nose, you would get it fixed simply to get out of pain. Why is emotional pain any different? If life mistreats you or something unwanted happens to you, why not heal the emotional pain the same way you would heal physical pain?

Traumatic life events do not have to become life sentences where we continue to carry around these heavy, emotional backpacks.

You can put down these backpacks as soon as you are ready and willing to let go.

New stuff can be created by our past experiences and our mental dialogue.

It's important to notice what we are telling ourselves on a regular basis and not take the mental narrator so seriously.

Once you have had a taste of the freedom this work can provide, it will be hard to go back to your old ways!

2

How to Magically Remove a Backpack

So how do we even begin to remove a heavy backpack? In this chapter, I introduce seven steps for removing any kind of backpack. Anybody who has the interest and desire can follow these steps to be free of the backpack. By practicing this technique, any kind of emotional stuff clears out like magic.

This is the real deal and can be pure magic when practiced in tandem with the other principles we will discuss in Chapters 3, 4, and 5. Together, these steps are the ingredients to clear out emotional turmoil and restore your peace.

The Technique

Steps 1 – 3 form the backbone of this technique which involves writing or stating a heartfelt request to God or higher power to have the emotional pain—the stuff—cleared out and released. Although you can make a verbal statement, it is often more effective to put the request in writing as this focuses the mind and the intention.

There are many criteria that must be present in order for this request to work successfully, which we'll further detail in Steps 4 – 7. In order for the technique to work, you will need to do some additional homework which has been outlined in the steps.

STEP 1: WILLINGNESS

I consider this the most important ingredient in clearing out stuff. You have to possess a true willingness to put the backpack down. Otherwise, the backpack isn't going anywhere and this method will not work. Mechanically asking to have the stuff cleared out or writing a letter will not get the job done.

In Chapter 6, under the section titled "The Greatest Obstacle to Clearing Out Anger and Other Forms of Stuff," I will relate a personal story illustrating how having willingness is a key ingredient even in the most challenging situations.

HOW DO YOU KNOW IF YOU'RE READY TO LET GO?

The good news is there's a simple test to see if you are ready to put down any backpack you may find yourself carrying. All you have to do is ask yourself if you are willing to let go and think about how that would feel.

If you are ready, the idea of letting go will manifest as feelings such as these:

- Welcoming
- Exciting

- Inviting
- Intriguing
- Exhilarating
- Energizing
- Appealing
- Enticing

If you are not ready to let go, on the other hand, you will encounter any of the following:

- You feel resistance
- Letting go feels forced
- You feel rushed and incomplete
- You feel fearful about letting go
- You feel as though your heart is unwilling to let go
- You feel opposed to the idea of releasing the stuff

In these instances, it means you will have some homework to do in Steps 4 to 7.

You can phrase this question in a number of different ways. It's not the form that is important. Ultimately, you are gauging how you feel in response to it. Think about the idea of letting go and how it makes you feel.

For example, you could ask yourself the converse question: *Am I willing to continue to hold onto this backpack?*

If the answer is yes, or if you feel fearful or anxious about the idea of letting go, then you are not ready to let go. And that's perfectly okay. You can't force yourself to be ready to let go. It may signify that you need to continue working on Steps 4 to 7 to help increase your readiness to let go.

If your answer is no, you have opened the door to mighty change. And this is deep and profound change—the kind that changes lives. You cannot begin to imagine the release you will experience once you put down these age-old burdens—many of which are too old to even calculate when they were first acquired.

The more you experience this work in action, the more your desire to let go of stuff will increase. Once you have just one experience of clearing stuff out, you will never again have the same tolerance for it. Once you have had just a little taste of freedom, picking up the backpack again will not seem as desirable.

WHY YOU MIGHT NOT WANT TO LET GO

You might be asking yourself, *why on earth would anybody not be willing to let go? Isn't this first step a given? Doesn't everybody want to let go of their stuff?* Theoretically, who in their right mind would want to continue to hold onto sadness, anger, fear, and other forms of pain and misery when there is a way out? The answer to this question can help us shed some light on why people won't let go so we can work through these resistances. Let's briefly discuss some reasons why people are sometimes unwilling to let go.

We mistake the stuff as part of ourselves. We've already discussed that it's impossible to put down the heavy backpack if we are unaware we are carrying it around in the first place.

We become accustomed to feeling the weight on our shoulders and believe there's nothing we can do about it. Being aware of the heavy backpack is not the same as acknowledging we have the power to put it down—that it is not a permanent part of who we really are.

We are so clogged up we don't even know where to start. Some of us have become so accustomed to being emotionally clogged up we wouldn't even know what it's like to "feel" again or how to work with our emotions.

We will often opt for what's familiar rather than replacing it with the unknown. Since change doesn't come easy for many people, it can be downright frightening to imagine letting go of stuff. After all, stuff can become a constant companion—what fills the lonely void and empty feeling when we're dealing with anger, sadness, or grief. Although our stuff might not be comfortable, it is FAMILIAR.

You are initially taking a leap into the unknown. But once you've had just one experience tasting the tremendous joy accompanying the release of your stuff, you will wonder why you didn't do it sooner. It's like being stuck for years in a dark, cramped room and walking out into the sunlight and fresh air. There is nothing to fear about such a positive change.

We can sometimes misuse emotions to feel alive or powerful again. Because our stuff cuts us off from our true source of power inside of us, we often resort to substitutes. We can misuse anger, for example, as a source of power. If we use anger as fuel to feel powerful and alive, we can become addicted to conflict—which we may be unwilling to let go of so quickly. If we are sad for so long that we have come to depend on that state of being, it might help us bond with others or even garner sympathy.

Real power comes from being in touch with the true strength we all have within us. Once we reconnect to this true source of power, we will no longer need these false replacements.

We can come to depend on our stuff as a part of our identity because it has been with us for so long. Suppose you were wronged or victimized in the past, and this gave rise to a tremendous amount of anger. It may be tempting to hold onto this anger and incorporate it into your self-identity. There might even be a part of you that enjoys telling people the story of how you were wronged and explaining to them how much you have been through and why you have a right to be so angry.

You can recall the experience without having to hold onto the anger. You also can heal those battle scars while still retaining the life experience and the lessons learned. Holding onto the stuff only continues to give rise to further suffering and can be released at a time of your own choosing.

Holding on helps us feel connected to the past. One of the more interesting reasons we hold onto stuff—such as grief after losing a loved one—is how it helps us feel connected to the past. We may actually feel as though the pain is an important part of the loved one we've lost and that clearing out the pain feels like letting go of our connection to this person.

Here again, you can still connect to the past without having to retain the hurt and the suffering. The love and connection you had to someone will always be there. Continuing to hold onto the suffering will not affect this connection one way or the other. Regardless of the circumstances surrounding someone's death, you always have a choice as to how long you continue to hold onto the pain. You decide when to face and let go of this kind of hurt.

> *The pain and hurt surrounding the situation and the person's death do not have to be forever interconnected.*

Regardless of the reason you are unwilling to put down the backpack, letting go always entails recognizing how much the stuff is wreaking havoc on your peace of mind, and recognizing that you desire peace over whatever you perceive that the stuff is giving you.

HOW BAD DO YOU WANT IT?

One cold and icy morning, my mother slipped on some black ice and broke her knee. A knee or "patella" break requires immobilizing the leg for about six weeks and keeping it completely straight following surgery. After this time, it requires an incredible amount of painful and intense physical therapy in order to bend the knee again and regain normal range of motion.

My mother was told that she might only regain 70 percent of her former range of motion. My mother is an extremely independent and active person. Living like this wasn't an option for her. She was determined to do everything she could to get her full range of motion back and resume her active lifestyle.

She attended physical therapy five days a week. Even on the "off days" she would still use the equipment that forced her knee to bend. She tirelessly worked out several times a day to strengthen her quadricep muscles and bend the knee joint. It was incredible to watch her dedication for almost six months!

While in therapy, my mother has met several people with similar injuries who stopped physical therapy after achieving a certain range of motion. They told her that physical therapy is very painful, tiring, and time consuming. They have, therefore, reached a point where they are satisfied enough with the results.

But my mother wasn't happy with regaining just 60 or 70 percent of her previous range of motion. With every fiber of her being, she wanted to regain as much range of motion as possible. As of this writing, which is six months following the injury, she has regained nearly 100 percent of her previous range of motion!

The point is, your results will be in direct proportion to your willingness to let go and your desire to experience true happiness. The more determined you are and the more desire you have to let go, the better your results will be.

Summing Up Step 1:

All requests and written letters asking to have the stuff cleared out must contain a true measure of willingness to let go of the stuff.

This is the most important ingredient in clearing out stuff.

STEP 2: ASK FROM THE HEART

The second ingredient necessary for freeing ourselves from our emotional backpacks: ask from your heart. Whether you choose to write or speak or think these intentions, they absolutely must come from a sincere desire to have the stuff cleared out. As we've touched on previously, if you pay lip service or merely go through the motions without truly desiring to clear out the stuff, you will not experience the incredible results we have been discussing.

The amount of sincerity you invest when asking for peace will greatly influence the results of clearing out the stuff. If it is sincere and heartfelt, you can truly move mountains.

HOW TO INCREASE YOUR DESIRE

One way to increase your desire and resolve is to think about how it would make you feel being stuck with those unwanted houseguests we discussed back in Chapter 1. We're not talking about a nice little analogy. What if it actually happened?

Picture yourself living with unwanted houseguests. Allow yourself to imagine the frustration this would create for you. How would you feel if someone wrongfully took up residence in your home? Would you feel angry? And how strong is your desire to tell these folks to leave?

Now, tap into that same level of frustration with harboring your stuff. Try to cultivate that same level of enthusiasm and desire to ask your stuff to leave. If you're having trouble accomplishing this, think about how long you have allowed your stuff to freeload within your house. Keep in mind that it has not only taken up residence, but the stuff has also decreased your peace of mind. Allow this frustration to fuel your desire and strengthen your willingness to let go and be free of your stuff.

Don't Force It

If you are feeling sad or angry about something, do not force yourself to write a letter or make a request to clear it. The best time to write a letter is when you are ready to have the hurt removed because it will come from the heart. Tap into the part of you that recognizes you are better off not holding on any longer and desires to experience some relief.

If asking to have the stuff cleared out feels premature or forced, don't try to make it happen. You may need to work on Steps 4 to 7 before you are ready and willing to let the stuff go.

Summing Up Step 2:

When making your request, you must have a true desire to clear out the stuff.

STEP 3: THE MAGIC OF STEPPING BACK AND LETTING STUFF CLEAR

The third step is magical. If you ask sincerely and have a true willingness to let go, you must then step back and let the stuff clear out. You need not have a clue how this will happen for you. When you write a letter or verbally ask to have the stuff cleared out, make sure you get out of the way and let the magic happen. Don't try to force anything to happen.

WHAT I LEARNED FROM AN EXERCISE MACHINE

Growing up, I recall seeing ads for an exercise machine that utilized something called "isokinetic resistance." Isokinetic resistance referred to the idea that the more force you use to push against the machine, the more force the machine uses to push back.

Suppose you are doing bench presses on this machine. The more forcefully you push up, the more forcefully the machine pushes down, and consequently makes you feel more weight. Throughout each repetition, you experience more uniform resistance because it mirrors the amount of force you are putting into the machine.

This is also the case when trying to clear out and release an emotion, especially after making a request to have the stuff cleared out. The more strongly you resist the emotion or try to force something to happen, the more power you give to it. It is only when you stop resisting the emotion and stop fighting that the emotion can begin to release.

Never *try* to make something clear out. Follow the steps here and write a heartfelt letter. Then, get out of the way and do nothing… and let the magic happen.

Yes, I know it sounds too good to be true; but I've seen it work in every conceivable situation. You do not have to understand the how and the why or what you will experience as the process unfolds. For now, I want to teach you the basic concept about making the request or writing the letter.

Note: In many cases, the last four steps must precede or accompany this work. These steps, which we will cover in a moment, are often necessary ingredients to help you be ready, able, and willing to let go.

———

IS THIS ALL YOU HAVE TO DO?

No. Sometimes writing down or saying a heartfelt request will suffice. However, in many cases, you must also do four other steps in order for the verbal request or letter writing to work its magic.

Summing Up Step 3:

After asking to have the stuff cleared out, it's important to let go and allow the magic to work.

Introduction to Steps 4 to 7: The Rest of the Steps

As previously stated, sometimes the request itself is not enough. The simple truth is we are not always ready or willing to let go. Therefore, we may need to do some preparation before we are willing to make a heartfelt request to have the stuff cleared out. The remaining four steps will help to increase our willingness and ability to let the stuff go and use the technique in all circumstances!

STEP 4: OPEN THE DOOR

It's not easy to get rid of unwanted guests if they are out of sight and hiding behind a locked door. Our stuff operates in the same manner. It's impossible to clear out stuff we have hidden away in an attempt to avoid confronting it. In fact, the letters and requests will have little or no impact. When emotions have been locked away for long periods of time, *they need to be let out before they can be cleared out.* Now is the time to open the door and allow the sunlight to come streaming in.

Sometimes, when we don't want to face our stuff, we lock it away in a room that nobody can enter—especially ourselves! We keep the door locked and the lights off because the idea of letting the light in seems too painful.

But no matter how scary and terrifying your stuff may seem, you ultimately have to open the door. Be willing to allow the cavalry to come inside and rescue you, to allow the magic to work. This can only be accomplished by opening the door.

Summing Up Step 4:

Open the door and allow your stuff to surface. We cannot work with our stuff if we lock it away or bury it somewhere deep within us. Opening the door invites the magic inside.

STEP 5: WALK RIGHT IN

Once you have opened the door, it's time to do the unthinkable: walk right in and take a look. How on earth do you walk right in and confront your emotional stuff? Just follow The Four-Part Recipe.

THE FOUR-PART RECIPE TO CONFRONTING YOUR STUFF

1: Stop Running

The first step to confronting an emotion is to acknowledge its presence. People are often carrying around vast amounts of pain they have not acknowledged. You know it's there on some level, but you don't want to recognize it. It's easier to just go on about your life and pretend it's not there.

It reminds me of when we have a project deadline looming on Monday, but we would rather spend our Sunday at a ballgame. We know we are dreading Monday, but for now we will simply relax and enjoy ourselves.

Many of us play a similar game when it comes to our stuff. To avoid confronting our unresolved emotions, we focus our attention on our jobs, children, and other activities and relegate our emotional backpacks to the background.

This first part of the recipe is asking you to stop what you are doing and recognize any hurt, pain, anger, or other form of stuff that you might be carrying. Stop diverting your attention long enough to acknowledge all the emotional stuff you have been avoiding regardless of what form it might take.

Maybe you lost a loved one and never fully confronted the hurt and pain, which you've continued to carry around with you. Perhaps you were mistreated by a loved one and have continued to carry the pain with you without ever acknowledging to yourself that it's there. You might be peripherally aware of the pain but haven't fully acknowledged its presence.

Stop what you are doing and, for the first time, look at the stuff. You might even want to speak directly to the stuff and say to it, "I see you." Avoid redirecting your attention elsewhere and acknowledge the emotions you have been carrying with you.

2: Experience It

It's not enough to just acknowledge that the pain is there. You must also allow yourself to experience it. This involves moving your awareness and attention into those areas that are hurting—allow yourself to experience them.

Focus your attention on these emotions and give them the attention they deserve. This involves getting quiet and still long enough to allow all the anger, sadness or other emotions to wash over you. Dive right into it and experience it.

In a nutshell, this step is asking you to move your awareness and attention into the areas of stuff you have avoided so you can fully experience these emotions.

Before doing this, it's important to remember the Wizard of Oz analogy mentioned previously. While the emotions might look intimidating and scary, remember there's just a harmless little old man sitting behind the curtain.

It's important to ask yourself if it's worth the temporary discomfort of confronting your stuff for the long-term gain of experiencing peace. This can often serve as a powerful motivator!

What I'm asking you to do is look discomfort right in the eyeball and don't back down. Move right into the pain without trying to resist it. Allow the full experience of your pain to surface and sit with it. Let them finally have their say. Allow yourself to experience the emotions that you have been working so hard to avoid.

3: Allow

There are no wrong reactions to experiencing your stuff. If you feel like yelling, crying, or screaming, that's fine. You might need to talk to your stuff and have a conversation. There is no right or wrong way to respond to your stuff. What's important is to recognize it and experience it. That alone will cause your stuff to unravel. This is often a vital and necessary part of the seven steps.

Don't be afraid to look your stuff right in the eyeball and allow yourself to feel and experience your emotions.

4: Remember the Help

While experiencing the stuff, keep in mind you will have plenty of help. After you have experienced the stuff and feel ready to let go, you can immediately ask to have the stuff cleared out.

SMELLY ROOM, ANYONE?

What if I told you that the next time you were angry, sad, or scared, you could have all of it quickly cleared out by going into a filthy, dirty, and foul-smelling room for a few minutes? Would you be willing to go?

I know it's an absurd question but how much would that be worth to you? What if it meant feeling wonderful and releasing all the things that are holding you back from feeling happy and peaceful? Yes, it sounds nuts, but that's the situation we find ourselves in when we need to confront our stuff.

Facing your emotions and confronting them is like having to walk into a smelly room. Is it unpleasant? Yes. Is it uncomfortable? You bet. But if it means the release of emotional turmoil, wouldn't it be worth it to you? Just as most people would be willing to walk into a smelly room if it could liberate them from the burdens they have been carrying around, it's also worth experiencing your emotions to bring about freedom from emotional suffering.

Most people aren't volunteering to walk into a smelly room. It would definitely be an unpleasant and unenjoyable experience. But the results can be nothing short of miraculous. The temporary discomfort is a small price to pay for the opportunity to release and heal the hurt, sadness, grief, anger, guilt, and other forms of stuff by acknowledging, experiencing, and feeling your stuff. After that, a simple letter or request can sometimes do the trick.

If you've never attempted this before, it's as easy and direct as it sounds. You walk up to the emotion and move right into it. Allow yourself to experience it. Remember that it's only stuff and can't hurt you even if it appears terrifying on the surface.

One of the main reasons people do not confront or experience their grief, anger, guilt, and hurt is because it scares them—they believe it will be too painful to bear. But it is the very act of NOT looking at your stuff that gives it power over your life. When you don't confront and acknowledge the pain inside of you, you allow it to thrive and continue to wreak havoc. On the other hand, the act of seeing and acknowledging your stuff initiates its transformation.

Remember to ask yourself this silly question: *Am I willing to walk into a smelly room in order to let go of the hurt I have been carrying around so I can feel more peaceful?*

If the answer is yes, then go for it. Walk right into your stuff. Walk into all of that anger, hurt, pain, and sadness that you are experiencing and allow yourself to feel it and experience it. It can't hurt you any more than a smelly room. But it can change your life.

I know that for some of you this might be the very first time you've ever attempted anything like this. Congratulations! This is a huge milestone in your life.

TEA TIME

I once had a teacher who taught me a simple concept of sitting down and "having tea" with my stuff. This has stuck with me to this day. "Having tea" entails sitting down and acknowledging my emotions and giving them the time and space they deserve. This taught me to sit and allow my emotions to have their say. It's not the quantity of time that's important, but the quality. It might only be a few minutes, but those few minutes can truly make all the difference between sadness and joy.

While you are having tea with your stuff, have no agenda other than allowing these emotions to exist and to be in your space, in the same way you might treat an old and treasured friend.

Don't be in a hurry. Do whatever feels natural. Cry, scream, laugh, sob, listen, feel, and observe. It's helpful to keep in mind you are experiencing the emotion for the purpose of letting it go rather than strengthening it. Acknowledge the emotions, express them, and feel them. Don't scrutinize these emotions or judge your response to them. Experience each emotion without trying to fight it or force it to do anything. Let the emotions wash over you.

It's also important to not get consumed with the emotion. You can still maintain a small part of yourself that is observing the emotion without becoming completely overtaken by it. This part of yourself can maintain the perspective that embracing, accepting, and allowing yourself to experience the emotion is ultimately how you will heal it. You can take as long as you like—a few minutes, a few hours, or longer. Set aside an evening to just sit with the emotions, which is something I have successfully used in my life. Just walk right in and allow yourself to experience every nuance, every flavor, and every subtle and not-so-subtle aspect of the emotion you are feeling. It bears repeating, don't try to fight it or force it to do anything.

Check in with yourself periodically and ask: *Am I willing to let go?* Now let's not confuse "having the willingness to let go" with "just forget about it." The situation itself will still be there. You may still be upset about it. Letting go of the pain surrounding the situation is not about forgetting what happened; it's about giving yourself permission to feel lighter and happier despite having to deal with an undesirable situation.

During the process, you will have a kind of inner knowing or you might feel a nudge deep inside encouraging you to let go of the hurt and pain. It might feel as though you have experienced the pain for long enough and are now ready to let go.

This is the ultimate dichotomy. You can live with unwanted and unpleasant situations and simultaneously release all the heavy emotions you carry, thereby allowing you to find peace.

Walking into our stuff is all it takes to initiate tremendous change. It opens the door for us to become more comfortable with the idea of letting go and making that all important request to have the stuff cleared out. When we can do this, we open up the space for the miraculous.

JUMPING IN THE POOL

I took swimming lessons as a child and can remember being absolutely terrified of jumping off the diving board. I thought that after countless lessons, maybe I could somehow perform this seemingly impossible task by the end of the summer. I would have never guessed in a million years what was coming next, nor will I ever forget that incredible day.

The swimming instructor had me stand at the end of the diving board. She wanted me to become more comfortable with it. As I stood there anticipating my next instruction, she did the unthinkable. Without warning, she quickly pushed me off the diving board! Astounded, I quickly began treading water and frantically swimming to the side to safety. It took a minute or two to process what had just transpired. *Did I just jump off (okay actually, I was pushed off) the diving board? Yes!* I was instantly hooked and couldn't wait to jump off the diving board again. I spent the rest of that hour jumping off the diving board and couldn't wait to show my mom!

It was a life-changing experience my instructor taught me—a five-year-old—that day. We could have stood on that diving board for months theorizing about jumping off. We could have had numerous lessons on exactly where to stand when jumping off a diving board and how to achieve the perfect stance and optimal form. We could have had countless demonstrations from professional divers showing us exactly how to do it. We could have read books or watched movies about proper technique and how to overcome the fear of jumping off a diving board. Ultimately, we can't sit around mentally dissecting how to jump off a diving board; we just need to jump. We need to take concrete action and actually immerse ourselves in the experience.

The same is true regarding our stuff. You can spend years and years talking about and analyzing your fears, anxiety, anger, and guilt—which is definitely an important part of the process we will discuss in Step 6. However, it's easy to get lost in the story surrounding the origin of your stuff and to forget that we need to experience our stuff so we can let it go. It's critical we do not get lost talking about our story without actually experiencing it. To clear out your stuff, you have to dive in it. Only by jumping into your stuff can you directly experience and connect with it. And once you directly experience your stuff and look it right in the eye, it loses its power over you.

We're not suggesting you avoid talking about your stuff. Sometimes, it's just not enough to talk about your stuff without allowing it to surface and experience it. For example, you can spend countless years talking to friends or a therapist, elaborating on and dissecting the situation in great detail. But despite years of conversation, you're still carrying the stuff with you. There is such a thing called analysis paralysis and, in this case, it's discussing your stuff over and over again without ever experiencing it.

In fact, I had a friend who spent close to $100,000 on therapy to work on unresolved feelings of anger from childhood, yet she remained angry. When I asked her if she had ever worked directly with the emotions and allowed herself to feel and experience them, she said she had only discussed them because experiencing the emotions seemed too painful. She said that taking medication helped her numb the pain so she wouldn't have to deal with the anger. Medications can be quite necessary in many situations, and only a licensed healthcare professional can make that determination. But it's also important to avoid falling into the trap of misusing medication to avoid confronting it.

It's easy to spend vast amounts of time accomplishing very little if you are not willing to actually experience the story. Detaching from your story does not bring forth the same kind of healing you can accomplish when you actually experience it. It's about getting your feet wet and being willing to jump in the deep end of the pool. This is where the technique of asking to have the stuff cleared out becomes incredibly effective and can help to clear out seemingly endless amounts of stuff. The point is to stop analyzing your story and to clear out the stuff that has been ruining your peace of mind.

Jumping in the pool can often bring about the change that years and years of standing on the diving board could not accomplish, allowing you to clear out intense, lifelong stuff. Now you can truly begin working with the magic of the seven steps and clear out any kind of stuff. Don't spend your life standing on the diving board. This work becomes miraculous once you take a leap of faith and jump into the pool.

We can still have our story and the lessons we learned. And we can also release and clear out the cause of all the suffering, which is the stuff we continue to hold onto.

But what if somebody is so numb that they can't feel ANYTHING?

EMOTIONAL CONSTIPATION

Before we conclude Step 5, I want to address an extremely important and related topic that can prevent you from being able to practice these techniques every time it is present. I briefly mentioned this concept earlier in the book. We'll delve into it more deeply here.

Billy and the Bathroom:

This is a story about my friend's son, Billy, who went through a phase of being petrified to go to the bathroom. For days on end, Billy would complain about having a stomachache. Due to his intense fear of going to the bathroom, he would be powerless to do anything about it. I remember thinking, *I wish he could understand how much energy he is expending by not going to the bathroom.*

Billy didn't have the insight to understand that a few unpleasant minutes of going to the bathroom could circumvent days and days of serious pain. And, so, the remedy he used to ease the stomachache was to hold it in and have his mother give him various medications that temporarily numbed and alleviated the pain.

Unfortunately, this scenario is similar to what many of us do to cope with our emotional pain. We decide that it's much easier to hold it all in and stop feeling anything rather than confronting our emotions. This is a very common pitfall we use when dealing with unpleasant emotions. Like Billy, we can end up resorting to various techniques to numb the pain. We can also expend tremendous amounts of energy holding on to stuff because it takes a lot of energy to harbor anger, sadness, guilt, grief, and fear. And since the stuff takes up a lot of our energy, it leaves us feeling tired, drained, and innervated.

Emotionally constipated people sometimes engage in such behavior as a coping mechanism for their stuff—as a temporary respite. Some resort to alcohol, medication, and recreational drugs because it temporarily numbs the stuff and provides a chance to relax. And some even use hobbies, such as travel or running, to distract themselves from the stuff. There are people who travel the globe to avoid having to deal with or experience all those hidden emotions they have been burying deep inside. To some, it may feel like planning their next big trip when in reality they are seeking the next big distraction.

Even sitting at home without plans can be difficult for some people as it requires being alone and forces them to come face to face with their stuff. Any vice we use to distract ourselves will never be enough—we'll constantly be planning another trip or coming up with the next big distraction. The problem with traveling to cope with your pain can be summed up in the age-old adage, "wherever you go, there you are." You can't run from your stuff since it is internal and, therefore, it follows you wherever you go.

If you aren't willing to crack open the door just a bit, the light can't enter. You are keeping all the help outside while you and your stuff remain locked inside. Be willing to relieve the emotional constipation. Be open to practicing the techniques we have been discussing.

It's important to understand that it's almost impossible to work with the techniques in this book and to clear out stuff when you have made yourself numb.

WHY ARE THERE SO MANY PEOPLE WITH EMOTIONAL CONSTIPATION?

Few of us have been taught to deal with our emotions properly, making it difficult for the majority of us to handle our stuff. That's why it's so easy to think of examples when emotional constipation might be a tempting solution. Suppose the pain of losing a long-term relationship is too much to handle. There are countless scenarios like this where people are ill-equipped to deal with the immense pain and therefore have to resort to unhealthy ways of coping with it.

Like my friend's son Billy, we might not even know we have been engaged in this behavior because we have been practicing it for so many years.

The Disconnect

Being emotionally constipated prevents us from truly connecting to life because all the stuff that has been hidden away dulls our senses—making life lose its vibrancy and excitement. We become numb and operate solely on a mental level with little or no emotion. Being emotionally absent makes it difficult to deeply connect with other people since we are no longer even connected to ourselves.

If you meet someone who is emotionally constipated, it can be very frustrating because it's nearly impossible to establish an emotional connection. Emotionally constipated people are usually most compatible with someone else who is also emotionally constipated since neither one is interested in connecting on an emotional level.

It's hard to be happy when you operate on such a one-dimensional level without really connecting to anyone else—including yourself. Even if you find yourself on a beautiful beach or experiencing a major life event, such as marriage or graduation, this emotional absence will cause you to feel detached and disconnected. You might have wondered why you felt so detached from everyone and everything, leaving you feeling so lonely. Even if you have lots of friends, avoiding the emotional connection will leave you feeling hollow.

Bad Side Effects

Suppose you stuffed all your trash under the door of a small locked room inside your house. For the time being, it would provide a temporary place for the trash, removing it from your immediate sight. However, the trash will still be there reaping some unwanted consequences.

As the garbage fumes overpower the little room, your entire house eventually stinks—and this is only the beginning. This filthy room begins to attract roaches, rodents, and other unwanted bugs and animals. Stuffing trash in this little empty room has now adversely affected your entire house.

Stuffing your emotions is much like this filthy room. It will always prove to have innumerable and unwelcome side effects. The peer-reviewed journals are replete with studies about how holding onto emotions and inadequately dealing with them can lead to self-destructive behavior. When you don't allow yourself to face and release these negative emotions, you might redirect them inward. You may now see yourself as the source of all of this pain and misery and, therefore, you want to lash out and do harm to yourself. This can sometimes lead to self-destructive behavior, which can mean self-injury or bodily harm to yourself including overeating, drinking, or suicidal thoughts.

Evidence also asserts that stuffing emotions can give rise to a variety of eating disorders and compulsions which you can find quite easily by searching the peer-reviewed journals online.

The point of the matter: when you push these negative emotions under the rug, a host of symptoms can emerge and manifest. We ignore our emotions at our own peril because this behavior carries significant risks.

THE WAY OUT

There is a way out of this seeming insanity. It begins with reversing this process. It is time to begin feeling again and accessing those parts of yourself that have been long denied. This will enable you to work with the techniques in this book and to clear out this fog that has been holding you down for so long. You can't work with the techniques in this book as long as you are emotionally constipated. How can you work with stuff when you can't even feel it?

The first step in this process is to work with the emotional blocks and eventually clear them out. We begin by listening to the emotions and feeling them within the body. The goal is to redirect your focus back to the body after years and years of avoiding it. This means really focusing on any and all feelings within the body, both physically and emotionally. When we become aware of what is happening within the body, we can start to reverse the process of ignoring our feelings and being perpetually numb. Many of us have disengaged from feeling anything within our own body, and this process can reverse it.

If you are someone who falls into this category, over the next few days I challenge you to become more aware of the emotions within your body, both physical and emotional. For some people, it's helpful to write it down and keep a record of your bodily feelings.

How do you feel right now? Do you feel tired, awake, exhilarated, sad, happy, or nervous? Are there any areas in your body that are hurting more than others? Is a part of your body feeling warm? Is another part of your body feeling cold?

Next, try to get more specific. You might feel heat in your left leg, a twinge of sadness in your heart area as you remember a loved one who has passed away, or anger being held within your stomach area. You might feel guilt, which is prominent in a specific location within your body. You might notice extreme tension in your left shoulder. Whatever it is, become more aware of these feelings within your body and bring more attention to it. We are attempting to move your awareness back into the body.

If you find it helpful, you can close your eyes and slowly work your way up through your entire body. Each time you reach a new area, move your awareness into that area and describe exactly what you are feeling.

Noticing all of these things will allow you to start the process of tuning back into your body. Bringing your awareness back to your body will enable you to begin feeling again and reversing this numbness and anesthesia you might have been living with for so long. Paying attention to your body will help you recognize how numb you have been for all of these years. Having this awareness is the first step in changing it.

This will allow you to take the giant step of opening the door to enable your stuff to surface. Once it surfaces, you can then confront it knowing full well that it cannot hurt you. Most importantly, you can begin the seven steps and rid yourself of all the stuff lying dormant in you—paving the way for happiness to return.

The bottom line:

You cannot stuff your emotions with impunity. You will always suffer the consequences in a variety of different ways. It is a lot simpler to face the emotions and let them go. This book offers an effective path to do this.

As for Billy, I'm happy to report that his story has a happy ending. After days of suffering, he finally went to the bathroom, and his pain mercifully came to an end. He no longer engages in this behavior and has since learned how much easier it is to simply go to the bathroom and move on with life rather than spending so much time and energy holding it in and numbing the pain.

You can do the same thing in your emotional life right now by taking the big yet simple step of opening the door and walking right in it. What are you waiting for?

Summing Up Step 5:

Allow yourself to feel your stuff again. Regardless of how scary it might appear, walk right into it and experience how it feels.

Once you've opened the door and walked right in, you have taken a mighty step towards some serious transformation. But there are still a few more things you need to do to clear the stuff out. Keep reading!

STEP 6: TIME TO TALK

Talking is another ingredient you might need before you are ready, willing, and able to sincerely ask to have the stuff cleared out. Talking is much like facing our stuff—they go hand in hand. The more we talk about something, the greater chance it has to process. The more we can process, the greater clarity and understanding we can gain about a situation before we are willing to let go. Mentally and emotionally processing your stuff is often necessary for letting go.

And that is the purpose of talking about our stuff. For many of us, it shores up our readiness to let go because it's easier to confront our emotions while we talk about the situation. Sometimes we can successfully ask to have something cleared out immediately. However, this may not always be possible, especially when it involves intense stuff. This is when friends, family, and professional counselors can come in handy; they can help us talk about our stuff, which makes it easier to reach a point where we are willing to let go.

TALKING AS A TOOL

In truth, talking about and understanding your stuff is NOT necessarily a prerequisite to letting it go. But, in many cases, it can be a necessary tool in developing the willingness to let go and allow the magic to work for you.

Suppose your boss just fired you. It's unlikely you're going to immediately ask to have all the associated emotions cleared out two minutes later. For heaven's sake, we would not be ready to let go of the emotions just yet. First, we would need to process what has taken place by talking about the situation and spending time with our emotions.

You might need to talk about your boss, the job, and all of your emotions surrounding being fired. You may need to express feelings of anger, sadness, or fear. These are all valid emotions, and it's healthy to talk about all of them. Whether you're expressing what you'll miss about the job or why you think the company made a mistake, the act of talking about it has tremendous therapeutic benefits. After you have given yourself sufficient time to talk about and experience the associated emotions, you will eventually have the desire to let go and make the request to have it cleared out.

GETTING THINGS OFF YOUR CHEST

Okay, we've all done it. We've all had a mental conversation with someone in our head in an attempt to get things off our chest.

Suppose your friend just chewed you out, and it completely took you by surprise. After your friend leaves and you have had time to digest the conversation, you come up with several comebacks you wish you had told your friend. You might imagine yourself doing it all over again—only this time you're telling your friend all these things you would have said.

Mentally rehearsing things that you would like to say to someone is a telltale sign that you need to speak your peace. The outcome is not as important. When you are having this mental conversation, it is common to become obsessed with what you should have said. You might also find it impossible to stop thinking about it—that you didn't speak your mind and tell this person what you were thinking when you had the chance. This means that you need to vent before you can write that letter.

Merely speaking your piece and getting these things off your chest will be extremely cathartic, allowing you to switch your focus to asking to have the stuff cleared out. In fact, getting things off your chest is sometimes the only way to unlock the door to successfully asking to have the stuff cleared out. It's not always easy to do and can also be terrifying to speak to someone and tell them how you really feel. At the same time, it can be incredibly liberating. In fact, it can be one of the most freeing things you will do in this life, and you will often feel a thousand pounds lighter after doing so.

At this point, any residual stuff can often clear out quite easily by simply asking to have it cleared out. By speaking your mind and getting things off your chest, you will greatly increase your readiness to let go, which is always the key to finding peace.

———————

SCARED OF SPEAKING YOUR MIND?

If you tend to get nervous and flustered while speaking your mind, I recommend taking the time to practice exactly what you would like to say and writing it down. It is helpful to pretend that the person is standing in front of you and you have the opportunity to express anything you want to them.

What would that look like? What exactly would you say? All you have to do is pretend you are speaking to them and see what happens. I actually like to talk out loud as though I was having a real conversation with the person. If you are uncomfortable with this, you can practice this exercise in your mind. Each time you practice mentally speaking to the person, more ideas will come forth. Be sure to write them down immediately.

When the perfect phrase or idea occurs to you, it's important you write it down immediately since it's easy to forget these fleeting ideas. It's easy to forget many of your key points because of nervousness or other emotions that sometimes get in the way. Therefore, it is vital to know exactly what you want to say beforehand. This will allow you to practice and rehearse the conversation and avoid getting sidetracked or missing out on the key things you want to express to this person. The goal is to say everything that is on your mind and get things off your chest so you can let go.

The Approach

When speaking your mind, you will be much more effective if you don't have an adversarial tone. It doesn't have to be confrontational and you can be diplomatic about it. You can accomplish this in many ways.

These two approaches are my favorite:

Option #1: Give Them a Heads Up

Convey to the person you feel there are things you need to say to them but specify that you would like to give them a chance to respond. You can even preface the conversation by saying you don't like dwelling on the past and holding onto things. Therefore, you would like to get some things off your chest by telling them exactly how you are feeling. Again, be sure to let them know that they are welcome to respond to anything that you say to them.

If this is a friend, family member, or coworker, you can preface the conversation by saying that you would like to improve your relationship with them. Tell them you are not trying to pick a fight with them but would like to express how you are feeling in order to help the relationship. This clears the way to expressing everything you want.

The goal is to talk and to get things off your chest. You do yourself a disservice by being consumed with anger and rehearsing lines you wish you could say to someone. Get it over with so you can move on with your life and get back to feeling good again.

Sometimes, merely saying the words and speaking your truth to someone will clear out tremendous amounts of stuff in and of itself.

Once you have said what you wanted to say, it becomes so much easier to ask or write a letter to have the stuff cleared out.

You might feel the need to express to someone that you are angry about how they treated you. Maybe you feel the need to know why they acted a certain way or what would cause them to say a particular thing to you. Whatever you want to say is valid. Stand up for your soul and say those things that will help to bring it peace.

Option #2: Write Them a Letter

If you really don't want to speak to someone, an alternative is writing them a personal letter which can be just as effective and cathartic. It allows you the opportunity to express exactly what you would like to say to this person without being interrupted and without the pressure of having them right next to you. In many cases, you may never have to send the letter! Writing and expressing your thoughts with the intention of sending a letter is sometimes enough to allow us to move forward and successfully clear out the stuff. By the time you finish writing the letter, you will feel a tremendous release and may have no interest in actually sending it.

The bottom line:

If you cannot stop thinking about what you want to say to someone, go ahead and tell them so you can move on with your life and clear out any pent-up stuff.

Summing Up Step 6:

Talking is often a necessary and vital component in achieving the willingness to make the request to have the stuff cleared out.

STEP 7: COMPASSION

When working with stuff, try not to judge it. Judging your stuff as good or bad stagnates the emotion and keeps it in place. Judgment is a form of resistance. Though we may be tempted to hate our stuff, and even despise it, giving it any energy at all can have adverse effects and prevent it from dissipating.

When you stop resisting and actively accept and generate feelings of compassion for your stuff, it begins to move again. If something doesn't clear for you and you have talked about the emotion and experienced it, sometimes having compassion for the emotion can do the trick. Then the request/letter writing can clear it out.

One way to have compassion for our stuff is to recognize it has every right to exist. It wants to express itself. It wants to be heard. If you honor the stuff and allow it to be, it will transform right before your eyes. If you judge it as wrong, you are essentially fighting the emotion, which only gives it more power over you and prevents it from clearing.

Try to feel compassion for the anger you are feeling. Try to console the grief-stricken parts of yourself. Try to give patience and understanding towards the fear. Work on recognizing you don't have to fight and forcibly remove the emotion. Allow it to be there and allow yourself to experience it. It's just stuff, and it has a right to be heard. The more you resist it, the more you are fueling and strengthening it. The more patience you have, the more rapidly it can clear.

If your stuff could talk, what would it say? What do you sense it wants to say? Maybe your anger is saying that you want to stand up to someone who has mistreated you. Or maybe your grief is saying how incredibly sad and alone it feels. There are no wrong answers here. The point is, we must listen to our pain and develop compassion for it. Try to have compassion for the parts of yourself that are suffering. Accept them emotionally rather than judging them as bad, wrong, or evil.

By having compassion on our stuff, we are having compassion on ourselves. It's okay to have compassion and love for those hurt parts of ourselves. It's all just stuff and deserves to be accepted. You can even visualize yourself giving your stuff a great big hug if it helps to generate compassion.

These are small and hurt children who need your love, compassion, and acceptance to transmute them back and restore your peace. You can reintegrate these hurt parts of yourself and allow them to become whole again.

This book is about reintegrating those parts of yourself that you thought were unlovable. The emotional energies that are just waiting for you to acknowledge them and clear them out are the very parts of yourself that need to be loved and accepted the most. Ceasing to fight and resist your pain is an extremely powerful step in clearing it out.

All of this might sound ridiculous, but I assure you that this can significantly alter the relationship we have with our stuff and transform the way we work with it. It's a game changer. Welcome your stuff the way you would a hurt or injured friend, pet, or child—with love and open arms. Seeing it through the eyes of compassion puts us in a state of readiness that allows it to be cleared out.

When you stop judging your stuff it magically becomes much easier to let go. And this allows the magic in Step 3 to work miracles.

COMPASSION FOR OTHERS

The second kind of compassion that can make a tremendous difference is having compassion for others. Sometimes when you are angry at someone and begin working with the seven magic steps, you will hit a wall. Even though you will clear out many layers of stuff, sometimes a kernel of anger still remains that can't seem to clear out.

One way to get past this hurdle is to have compassion for others, recognizing that they too are on the same journey and trying to do the best they can. Some people might have had a tougher upbringing than you or encountered challenges that have made them act the way they do. Looking at someone through the eyes of compassion can often mean the difference between holding onto anger or achieving the willingness to let go.

SUN AND RAIN

One way to avoid falling into the trap of hating your negative emotions and judging them as wrong or bad is to ask yourself if you hate the rain. After all, the rain sometimes ruins weekend plans and vacations.

Imagine if a technology existed that could stop the rain. If it started to rain, this technology would intervene and literally dissipate the clouds and the sun would return. At first glance, this sounds like a wonderful idea. No more spoiled picnics or weekend plans. No more rained out ballgames, pool parties, or days at the beach. No more windshield wipers or umbrellas.

But eventually there would be a day of reckoning as we would quickly realize that suppressing the rain is not a good idea. Drought would rapidly set in, not to mention the numerous other deleterious effects this would have on the atmosphere. Water from the ocean evaporates into clouds and returns to the ocean as rain in a system known as the hydrologic cycle. Without this system in place, ecosystems would cease to function normally. Plants and trees would die, rivers and streams would dry up, and life would cease to function normally. Our entire planet would rapidly become out of sync, upsetting the natural balance and order and leading to chaos.

Both the sunshine and the rain are vital components of the same system. Without the rain, life as we know it would perish. Anyone who has ever experienced a drought will readily tell you that during those times rain truly becomes a beautiful thing.

In the same manner, when you decide that your negative

emotions are bad and you try to suppress them, you are upsetting the natural balance. This imbalance will lead to countless problems that can manifest in numerous ways through a variety of symptoms.

Just as lightning and thunderstorms dissipate a tremendous amount of pent-up energy in the atmosphere and allow the sun to return, our negative emotions offer us a way to dissipate pent up energy within our own system. Allowing expression of these emotions returns us to a state of peace and enables the sun to return.

Rain is a necessary part of our lives. It's not good or bad, it just is. We can even learn to love and appreciate the rain. In fact, many people do. It's just a part of our experience here on earth. If we only experienced sunny days, we wouldn't have the capacity to notice the sunshine. It is only by experiencing the contrast of rain that we can truly learn to appreciate sunshine.

Positive and negative emotions are opposite sides of the same coin. They are both a necessary and vital component of your emotional makeup as a human being. Think of them as the rain; you can learn to appreciate your negative emotions as much as the positive ones—which is a necessary part of the total human experience.

When viewed through this lens, it becomes much easier to work with the techniques outlined in this book and to have compassion on your emotions. Be patient with them and allow them to have a voice.

Summing Up Step 7:

Try to have compassion on your emotions and do not judge them as good or bad. This allows you to stop resisting them so they can clear out. See your emotions as the rain, which is a necessary part of the human experience. Appreciating the rain as you work with these seven magic steps can lead you back to the sunshine.

CHAPTER 2 SUMMARY

When you write or make a heartfelt request to have any kind of emotional heaviness or pain cleared out, it will be successful if all the ingredients are present.

You must ask from your heart and have the willingness to let go. There are many reasons someone might not want to let go.

Use the litmus test we discussed to determine if you are ready to let something go or if you need more work. Ask yourself: *Am I willing to let go?* Then, notice how you're feeling: Do you feel blocked with resistance or open and energized?

We cannot clear out intense stuff until we face and confront it. This involves allowing the emotions to surface and confronting them using the techniques we have discussed.

Sometimes, talking about emotions is a necessary ingredient to obtain the willingness to let go. In some cases, there are things we must say to someone in order to obtain the willingness to let go. The techniques we discussed can help you articulate these unresolved things.

Try to see your emotions with compassion and acceptance rather than judging them as wrong or bad.

"Smelly Room," "Tea Time," and "Jumping in the Pool" are all important concepts that can give us the courage to move forward when confronting our stuff.

Use the guidelines we discussed to write a letter or make the request (explained in more detail in the next chapter) to have stuff cleared out.

The Seven Steps

1) Willingness

2) Ask from the Heart

3) The Magic of Stepping Back and Letting Stuff Clear

4) Open the Door

5) Walk Right In

6) Talk

7) Compassion

3

The Magical Request

HOW TO MAKE THE REQUEST

So far, we've established that one of the most important ingredients of this work is a heartfelt handwritten, spoken or typed request to have the stuff cleared out. We've also discussed the additional ingredients that are often necessary for using this technique including opening the door and experiencing the stuff, talking about it, and having compassion for it.

Once you are ready, how do you write a letter or verbally state your request? What do you say? How do you say it?

As long as you have the ingredients we discussed, the format and structure are secondary. If you have a sincere desire to have the stuff cleared out and a willingness to let it go, then you have two of the main ingredients in place. You can then successfully work with the steps we have been discussing in this book and write the letter. You can be as informal as you would like. You need to state your desire to have the stuff you are dealing with cleared out.

When you ask to have your stuff cleared out, it cannot fail. It is the one request in all the Universe that works every single time if all the ingredients we have been discussing are present. If you ask sincerely and are willing to let it go, you make way for the miraculous to unfold.

GUIDELINES AND EXAMPLES FOR
WRITING YOUR LETTER

Who?

First off, who do you write the letter to? You can address the letter any way that feels appropriate at the moment. In fact, you can make this request to whomever or whatever you want. You can address it to the Universe, the All that Is, your Higher Self, Guardian Angels, God, the Creator, the Holy Spirit, or any other term you feel comfortable using. You can change it up as often as you like.

It is not the words that are important but the intention behind them. Are you sincerely asking from your heart to have the stuff cleared out and are you really willing to let it go? The most important ingredients are the desire and willingness to clear the stuff out.

Don't let the absurdity fool you. This is the real deal and is pure magic when practiced in tandem with all the seven steps we have been discussing. Taken together, these steps are the ingredients to clear out any kind of emotional turmoil and restore your peace.

I usually change the wording and address of the letter depending on what feels the most appropriate at the time.

How?

Should you write it, type it, state your request aloud, or merely think about it mentally? This comes down to personal preference and what makes you the most comfortable. Sometimes you might prefer to write or type the request, while other times you may wish to state it verbally or think about the words in your mind.

I actually prefer to type a letter. At times, I believe that it can be much more effective than saying the words. For some of us, putting something into writing can help focus the mind and increase our intention. When I write a letter, my personal preference is to type it on a computer. After the letter is written, it's up to you to keep or delete it.

For many years, I typed letters each day. More recently, I have also opted to verbally or mentally focus on the request by stating my desire to be free of the stuff. Either way, the results have been spectacular. The letter writing has been my consistent favorite for the past ten years.

Remember, the key is to be focused and to put attention and desire into the words. The actual format is secondary to your intention.

General or Specific?

When writing or thinking these requests, you can either use the generic term "stuff" or specifically spell out the exact kind of stuff you would like to have cleared out, such as anger, rage, sadness, grief, fear, and so on.

You may choose to be extremely detailed about the apparent problem and the kind of emotions you are feeling or you can be vague about the situation, only asking to have the stuff cleared out. There is no right or wrong way to do this since it's not about the words but the intention and the willingness to let go.

Here are some simple and basic examples:

Dear Creator,

I am experiencing a lot of heavy stuff right now and I am asking you to clear it out.

Clear out all of this stuff that I now feel. Please clear it out completely and totally and bring me peace.

I am opening the door and invite you in to clear it out for me because right now I feel stuck.

I know that I have no clue how to clear this out and ask that you do it for me.

I am willing to let it go and ask for your help in returning to peace.

I ask to have all of this stuff cleared out because I am now ready to let it go.

Thanks.

Love,

Joey

You can step up the detail and include something like this:

Dear Higher Self,

I feel a lot of anger right now. Please completely clear out this anger that I am feeling in my heart and allow me to feel the underlying peace. I am asking to have this anger cleared out as I am now willing to let go of it and would like to be free of it. I invite you to come into this anger and take it away for me.

Thanks.

Me

Sound absurd? Do you really care if it leaves you feeling spectacular?

Always remember the words are not as important as the underlying intention.

Are you sincerely asking to have the stuff cleared out and are you willing to let it go? These intentions are what we are after when writing the letter or making the request. Focus on your intention to have the stuff cleared out leaving you feeling clear and joyous.

You don't need to know how this will be accomplished. Asking from your heart, coupled with a willingness to have it cleared out while you sleep, is nothing short of miraculous.

I often continue to write something along these lines for several minutes, asking to have the stuff cleared out. Each sentence affords another opportunity to express my heartfelt desire, intention, and request to have the stuff cleared out.

You can continue to write the same things over and over again for as long as it feels helpful.

Things will begin feeling lighter when you ask with the proper intention. After several minutes, it's important to stop writing and let go.

In Chapter 4, we will discuss exactly what happens after you complete the letter and how the entire process unfolds.

THE POWER OF SLEEP: A LIFE CHANGER

One of the most powerful ways to move mountains with clearing your stuff is to write a letter or make a request before you go to sleep. The results of using this technique as a ritual before you sleep can be astonishing.

Sleep provides us with a tremendous opportunity to make requests and then completely get out of the way. When we ask to be worked on while we sleep, this enables the magic to work on us throughout the night. We can clear out anxiety, anger, and fatigue in our sleep. The amazing truth: *You never have to wake up feeling the same way you did when you went to sleep.*

When you make a clear request to have your stuff cleared out and are truly willing to let go, you will receive the help you need. It's in the practicing of these techniques that the tremendous value of this work will shine forth and be recognized. All you have to do is ask:

- Ask from your heart to have the stuff cleared out while you sleep.

- Ask to be worked on throughout the night while you sleep—freeing you from the anger, grief, guilt, fear, or any other form of stuff that has been weighing you down.

Even if you are dealing with something intense, simply continue writing the letters each evening asking to have the stuff cleared out while you sleep, and each morning you will awaken much clearer. Even if the emotions return, you will notice they will return less intense—as though the volume had been turned down.

Each night before I go to sleep, I write a letter asking to have my stuff cleared out while I sleep. I ask to be cleared out throughout the night and to awaken clear and joyous. No matter how I feel when I go to sleep, I always wake up feeling clear.

It's so tremendous, it bears repeating:

You never have to wake up feeling the same way you did when you went to sleep.

I know it sounds miraculous. That's because it is miraculous! I know it sounds incredible. That's because it is incredible! This work is truly life changing regardless of whether or not you believe in it. You do not have to understand how this will be accomplished. You do not have to understand the "why" for this technique to work.

In Chapters 4 and 5, I outline my night-time letters process and how I have successfully used them in my own life to work through some very intense stuff. Those chapters will also clarify exactly how the process will unfold. For now, I encourage you to focus on practicing the techniques with an open mind and experiencing the incredible results firsthand.

Before you to go sleep, you could write a letter or mentally focus on an intention as simple as this:

Dear Creator,

Please work on me while I sleep and clear out all of this anger that I am feeling.

Work on me all through the night and clear out all of this stuff. Wake me up feeling clear and peaceful. I invite you to come into this sadness and work on it while I sleep. I am ready to let it go and would like to have it cleared out.

Work on clearing out all of this stuff/anger/sadness [or anything else you want to specify].

You could conclude with something like this:

Help me to fall asleep quickly and easily. Help me to sleep through the night in peace, waking up feeling clear and joyous.

Remember that it's okay to write the same thing over and over. The point is not to write a masterpiece. The goal is to express your sincere desire to have particular forms of stuff cleared out.

RISE AND SHINE

I also recommend writing letters each morning to clear out any stuff that got activated during the previous night. We process a lot while we sleep and can feel the activated stuff the next morning. If you have any residual emotion, you can ask to have it cleared out.

Writing a letter in the morning can leave you feeling more awake, invigorated, and emotionally clear. A good method is to go through each area of your body and systematically ask to have that area or region cleared out.

This short and simple exercise can leave you feeling more awake and energized each morning. Following the letter, I always enjoy a brief period of quiet or meditation before starting my day.

Dear _____,

Clear out all of this stuff that was triggered during sleep.

Clear out all of this stuff that I am feeling right now and work on me all through the day.

Thanks,

Joey

You can then spend a few moments in silence or meditation if you wish, or simply start your day.

———————

THE CEO MINDSET

Here's a final word on an attitude that can sometimes help us shift our focus into a state of mind conducive for clearing out stuff.

Suppose the chairman of the board wants to make a policy change within his or her power. The chairman can accomplish this quite easily without having to become angry or receive permission from the board. The chairman can issue the request and the board can take necessary steps to carry out the change.

You are in a similar position of power with your stuff. You can produce powerful results if you are cognizant of the fact that you are fully in charge of your inner environment. This recognition must come from a place deep inside where you truly understand that you have the power to rid yourself of unwanted stuff.

Like the chairman of the board, I will often tell my stuff to leave while I'm in this powerful state of mind. I don't ask or request that it leave, I confidently tell it to leave knowing full well that it must comply. When I do this, I will usually notice the stuff lightening up almost immediately. Directly addressing your stuff and asking it to leave can be extremely effective when it comes from a place that truly recognizes that you have the final say on what gets to stay and what must go.

It's important that we try to reframe how we see ourselves in relation to our stuff. We are at home while our stuff is the imposter. If we think in these terms, we can bring a lot more power and authority into our interactions with stuff. And when we write letters from this perspective, they are much more powerful and contain a stronger desire and request for our stuff to vacate the premises.

When you speak to your stuff while in this powerful state, you can often create real change in the way you feel. Don't forget this powerful way of working with stuff.

No matter how things may seem, never forget who is really in charge. You are eternally in the driver's seat while your stuff will always be the passenger.

CHAPTER 3 SUMMARY

You can write, speak, or visualize your request to have the stuff cleared out.

The most important ingredients are the intense desire to have the stuff cleared out, coupled with a true willingness to let go.

Writing or typing the request can often yield better results because it helps to focus the mind and increase intention.

You may address the letters to God or any other word that resonates with you.

Writing letters at bedtime asking to have the stuff cleared out while you sleep can be absolutely miraculous.

You never have to wake up feeling the same way you did when you went to sleep.

4

How the Magic Unfolds

You've successfully written a letter or made a request asking to have the stuff cleared out and have worked through the seven magic steps. Congratulations! Now what? What should you be doing? How long will it take for the stuff to clear out? What will you experience? In this section, we will discover how the magic unfolds.

WHAT TO DO AFTER WRITING A LETTER?

You can do anything to take your mind off of the stuff. Read a good book. Take a nap. Watch TV. Call a friend. Do anything that diverts your attention away from the stuff while making sure you avoid trying to make anything happen.

The reason for diverting your attention is that forcing a release will only make you hold on tighter.

For this reason, Step 3 of the seven steps requires us to let go and get out of the way. One of the best ways to accomplish this is to find something else to do! This helps you to let go and not force anything to happen, allowing the magic to go to work.

There's an old expression: "Whatever you resist persists." That is certainly the case when it comes to letting go of stuff.

You made the request or wrote a heartfelt letter with the desire and willingness to let go of the stuff. Now is the time to step back, breathe, and let go while the stuff automatically clears out for you. The good news: if you wrote from your heart and are truly willing to let go, the rest is magic.

———————

BECOME AWARE

The second thing to do is notice any changes you feel in your body and your emotions. For example, you might feel your emotions lighten and your breathing become deeper as the stuff releases. Sometimes it is dramatic and feels as though a ton of bricks is lifting off of you. All the anger, sadness, or other emotions you were previously experiencing feel as though they have lifted off of you. Other times, you will notice more subtle changes as the emotions gradually become lighter and you start feeling better. You might notice that a specific area of your body feels lighter.

For example, suppose you feel a heavy sadness in your chest area. You might notice these emotions getting lighter or even going away completely. You might even feel like taking some deep breaths as you begin feeling more relaxed.

The more you work with the magic steps, the more aware you will become of the many changes that take place when doing this work. We will discuss the changes you will feel in more detail in Chapter 8 along with some additional actions you can take to help the stuff clear more effectively.

For now, the letter has been written and released. Continue to let go and simply become aware of your emotions.

HOW LONG UNTIL THE STUFF STARTS CLEARING: A ROADMAP

Now it's time for the million-dollar question: Exactly how long will it take for the stuff to start clearing? How will the changes begin to manifest in your life? The answer to these questions actually depends on a few different factors. Without further ado, let's look at a roadmap of what you can expect when utilizing this work and putting these techniques into practice.

Stuff can clear out in different ways and can take varying amounts of time to do so. These are common experiences that could occur for you after writing a letter.

INSTANT GRATIFICATION

This is one of my favorites. Imagine asking from the heart to have your stuff cleared out and having it instantly vanish. Many times, that's exactly what happens. The emotion clears out right there on the spot. It is quite dramatic when it clears this way as you can literally feel the stuff lift off of you as you become markedly lighter during or shortly after the request. If this happens on your first attempt, you will be a fan of this work for life.

If it was a sincere request, you will often experience some sort of change or shift in how you feel almost immediately. I often write letters and experience a shift while I'm still writing. I notice that the emotion I was experiencing either becomes much lighter or vanishes altogether. I typically write the same phrases repeatedly for several minutes until I feel the stuff begin to clear out. I focus intently on the words.

The same goes for anger. When you're angry at someone and you ask to have the anger cleared out, it will sometimes clear out immediately and you will no longer feel the anger. You might have to continue to deal with the situation that caused your anger, but the actual angry feelings will have been cleared out. In this instance, when stuff clears out immediately, it will never return. That particular energetic pattern associated with that emotion is considered cleared out and said to be "healed." In these instances, nothing further needs to be done. You asked to have the stuff cleared out and... Voila! It clears out.

But this is not always the case.

DELAYED RESPONSE

This second scenario is where you experience a slightly delayed response without the instant gratification mentioned previously. Suppose you are furious about something and write a letter to clear it out. You might feel lighter while writing the letter, but you may continue to feel the stuff. That's okay. Don't panic. Find an activity, such as reading, watching TV, talking on the phone, taking a nap, playing sports, or any other activity to divert your attention away from the anger. As my mom always said, "Good things come to those who wait."

As your stuff clears in this manner, you will gradually start feeling lighter and clearer. It might be so subtle that you can't pinpoint the exact moment when things begin to shift. You might suddenly notice your stuff feeling lighter and you feel much better.

In my experience with this, I choose to watch TV or do something that takes my mind off of whatever is bothering me at the moment, and I try to let go of the process. What I subtly begin to notice is my breathing deepening and things are starting to feel much lighter.

OVERNIGHT

The next scenario requires an overnight clear out, which will often do the trick. Suppose you had an intense argument with someone. You are angry about it, and you just can't seem to let go. You are so worked up that it just won't clear out despite you writing a heartfelt letter. You've talked about. You've faced the anger. Felt it. Walked right into it. You have arrived at a point where you are willing to let it go but it just won't leave.

Sometimes you have to do "an overnight." This is where you write a sincere and heartfelt letter before you go to sleep and ask to be cleared out while you sleep. Think of it as dropping off your car at a service center and arranging to pick it up the next day. Major changes will happen while you sleep.

It's not important what you say, rather *how* you say the words—with honesty and intention.

Be prepared. Things will happen while you sleep. You might feel things shifting inside of you and, if you are sensitive enough, you might actually feel energy moving within you. In many instances, you will wake up feeling miraculously lighter and clearer. I often feel like a different person the next morning. It will be hard to imagine how you could feel so much better in such a short period of time. It will be equally hard to understand just how terrible you were feeling the previous night and are now feeling so much lighter and clearer. The difference will astound you.

This third scenario is also something you can do every single night of your life as we've touched on earlier in the book. Everyone stresses about something at night since the simple act of living each day facilitates stress. Stress often leaves us with unresolved stuff each night, which was activated during the day. Writing a letter before bedtime assures that this is taken care of while we sleep, and we can wake up refreshed and clear. As I stated earlier, you never have to wake up feeling the same way you did when you went to sleep.

INTENSE EMOTIONS AND TRAUMATIC LIFE EVENTS

For intense or traumatic events, it might require a longer period of time to clear out. This opens up a much broader discussion of the process of clearing out stuff. The next section will elaborate on how to clear out intense and traumatic stuff, and how this ties in with the lifelong process of clearing out stuff.

PEELING THE ONION: PUTTING IT ALL TOGETHER

If something is especially intense or emotionally charged, you might need several days, weeks or—in some instances—months to process and clear it out. In these cases, there are often multiple layers of stuff that need to be cleared out, one layer at a time. To describe this process, I like to borrow the term "peeling the onion" to describe how it unfolds. This process will usually involve all the seven steps and is often ongoing.

Shannon and Her Dog

Here's a story about my friend Shannon and her dog.

Shannon's dog had been with her for 14 years and had helped her through many rough times in life. The two had a close bond which left Shannon truly heartbroken when her dog passed away.

Shannon's usual pattern was to become withdrawn when she was sad.

She would often wallow in her pain for long periods of time. To avoid having to deal with her emotions, Shannon would suppress and bury the pain. However, this time was different.

Because Shannon and I had been good friends for several years, I knew her past behavior well. I knew she was interested in this kind of work, so I asked her if she would like to try something different. She readily agreed.

Right at the outset, I did not allow her to muck around in her misery. Instead, I convinced her to allow her emotions to come up and experience them. We talked about her feelings at length. We spoke about the hurt she was feeling, how much her dog meant to her, and other aspects about her precious dog. Incredibly, Shannon allowed herself to touch and feel her grief. She cried about her pain and spoke about the loss.

Next, Shannon wrote a sincere and heartfelt letter before she went to sleep that night. In the letter, she asked to have the hurt and sorrow cleared out. After I spoke to her at length, she recognized that letting go of her pain wouldn't bring her dog back or change the situation, but it would make her feel much more at peace.

The following day, there was a noticeable shift. She looked much better and commented that she was feeling lighter. Over the next few days, she continued to talk about her feelings and write the daily letters, especially before bedtime. Two days later, she was clearly in a much better place. The change was dramatic. She continued doing the work, and each day she appeared noticeably lighter.

There is no question Shannon will always miss her dog and feel tremendous sadness about the loss. What Shannon realized, she no longer had to hold onto the grief and suffering. Though Shannon couldn't change the situation, she successfully cleared out the heavy grief and sadness surrounding her. She no longer had to walk around enveloped by these dark, heavy clouds. While what happened will never be a pleasurable memory, Shannon can return to her peace. She can go about her day, feel joy and connected to life—and she can still miss her dog. No longer is her joy obscured by a heavy cloud, as she was able to clear it at a moment of her own choosing.

By not resisting or fighting the hurt and sadness, and instead allowing it to surface and just be, Shannon could have compassion for her emotions rather than judge them. She had recognized that the stuff couldn't hurt her. The very act of seeing and experiencing it went a long way towards healing it. She cried and mourned with the purpose of allowing her emotions to express outward rather than trying to hold onto the sadness and push it further inward. And, of course, each day she asked in her letters to have the hurt and sadness cleared out with a true willingness to let it go.

She ultimately realized that she had a choice and was cognizant of what she was choosing. She chose to move through it quickly and, as early as the next day, she said she began feeling much clearer and lighter. Several days later, she felt a ton of bricks lifted off her shoulders. I could visibly see the incredible contrast when looking at her.

CLEARING OUT STUFF ONE LAYER AT A TIME

When an emotion or life experience is intense, it is a process whereby you clear out one layer at a time. Each time you clear out a layer, you will feel lighter. This is how you will work through your stuff even when it is really intense emotional pain – by clearing it out one layer at a time. Each time you clear out another layer of stuff, it will return with less intensity and a little less noise. In Shannon's example, each time the grief would return, it felt more distant to her—as though the volume had been turned down. Since it lacked its original intensity, it was much easier to manage.

The more stuff you clear out, the easier it is to handle the next layer of stuff that arises because much more of you is now sitting in the sunlight. The more clouds that clear, the brighter you become. And when you are brighter, it is much easier to deal with the clouds when they return. As an added bonus, each time you clear out another layer, the next layer will not always immediately return. You may experience times where you feel happy and peaceful long before the next layer of stuff arises. It's as though each time you are temporarily removing the clouds, you allow the sun to shine for a bit before the clouds return again.

During this period of sunshine, you will feel much lighter and happier before the next layer returns. And when the clouds return, they will only cover about 80 percent of the sky, thereby allowing more light than before. This makes the return of the clouds easier to deal with as they are a little less intense. And when you clear out the next level of stuff, they will return with only 70 percent of the sky covered, making the stuff much more tolerable and less dark than when you first started. When you clear out this next layer of stuff, you will once again bask in the sunshine of your true self, allowing you to feel good again. And this time the clouds might stay away even longer before they return again. If they do return, perhaps only 50 percent of the sky is covered so they don't seem quite as dark as before and are less intimidating because of the additional sunlight of your true self. You will therefore feel less overwhelmed with the sadness, grief, anger, or any other form of stuff that you are currently experiencing. Initially, we might only have a brief respite to enjoy the sunshine before the clouds return. But as we continue to clear out our stuff, as it arises, we will notice longer and longer spaces between when the stuff clears out and when it returns. If you stick with the process and continue to clear out layer after layer of stuff, your life will dramatically change. The stuff will get lighter and lighter and no longer feel like a mountain of bricks on your shoulders. You will spend longer and longer periods in the sunshine, experiencing the joy of your true essence and how life feels without your stuff. Eventually, the stuff will stop returning altogether because all of it will be cleared out. At this point, there is nothing left but sunshine.

Ultimately, we are peeling the onion when we clear out our stuff. Layer by layer, we get back to our true essence: peace and joy. I believe this is one of the most important jobs we have in this life: to change darkness into light, one layer at a time. We are removing layer after layer of the illusion of who we thought we were. We thought we were the pain, fear, sadness, and guilt. And as we identified with our pain, it's as though we created a "false self." Incredibly, underneath this unhappy false self we've created lies the joy I have repeatedly mentioned throughout this book. It is our task to recognize the darkness and let it go. Only our belief in it has kept it in place. Once we wake up and recognize who we are, we can ask the stuff to leave and uncover the peace that has been with us all along.

What if you find yourself faced with serious, overwhelming grief? Can the techniques work even in this situation? How exactly does this work unfold? What can you expect from the overall experience? In the next chapter, we'll cover how I truly had to put these principles to the test to help me move through tremendous amounts of grief, sorrow, and other forms of stuff.

CHAPTER 4 SUMMARY

After writing the letter, sit back and let go. Find something else to do and stop trying to force anything to happen. This allows you to get out of the way and let the magic happen.

Watch TV, read, or engage in any activity that takes your focus away from the stuff you are trying to clear.

Notice any changes you feel, such as the emotion becoming lighter or disappearing completely. You might also notice yourself feeling calmer or breathing more deeply.

Clearing out stuff can be an instantaneous process or unfold gradually over hours, days, or longer periods of time. Sometimes, it will clear out almost immediately and never return. On other occasions, it will take a little longer until you subtly notice yourself feeling much calmer and peaceful.

Other times might require you to write a letter before you go to bed (I encourage this every night), asking to have the stuff cleared out. In these cases, you will often feel much lighter in the morning.

Most times, it is a process by which you clear out a little more stuff each day. Each time it returns, it will come back lighter, as though the volume is being turned down. You will feel much lighter and the stuff will feel less overwhelming.

As a bonus, you might also experience a joyous absence of stuff before the next layer returns. And, when it returns, it will be noticeably lighter than it was previously.

If you stick with it and continue to clear out each layer that arises, it will gradually lighten up tremendously and disappear entirely.

5

Grief, Death, and Magic - My Story

THE ULTIMATE TEST

I had a tremendous opportunity to put the principles and techniques in this book to the test when I experienced my father's tragic and prolonged illness. My dad was a wonderful, kind and caring man who was everybody's friend. He never met a stranger. He was friendly with adults and children alike. In fact, my mom would often refer to him as the Pied Piper since he had such a vast array of friends of all ages. All the children in the neighborhood truly adored him.

Our house was always the place where all the neighborhood kids would come to hang out. They not only came to play with me, but also my father. My dad was a big kid at heart and just one of the guys. All the kids in the neighborhood were on a first name basis with him. In fact, I remember a time during my youth when my mom shared a story about how a kid knocked on the front door during summer vacation to ask: "Can Norman come out and play?"

I have fond memories of my father. He was one of those people who always enjoyed what he was doing. Whether he was eating, watching TV, or socializing, he would savor the experience. He knew how to enjoy life, no matter how great or insignificant the activity.

With my father, I could laugh and joke about virtually anything. His happy-go-lucky attitude and ability to enjoy life made it easy to have a good time doing almost anything. He had an uncanny ability to just let things slide off his back. He rarely stressed about anything and could always make you feel better.

We could have never guessed what awaited my father and the suffering he would endure. In his late 50s he began suffering from a progressive, degenerative, neurological illness that took everything away from him—from the ability to speak to fine muscle coordination—a little bit at a time, over the course of several years.

Needless to say, watching my father slowly deteriorate triggered a tremendous amount of stuff for me. Grief, sadness, guilt, and fear were just some of the emotions I experienced throughout the process.

First off, it seemed so frightening to think of life without my father. He was the rock of our family. He was always the person to turn to for advice and had single-handedly built our family insurance business. He was a tremendous decision maker with a keen insight for knowing exactly how to deal in almost any given situation. The thought of not having him around was almost inconceivable.

Equally intense was the grief that arose as I watched my father slowly deteriorate. It was gut wrenching to watch and gave rise to the greatest inner darkness I have ever known. One of the first things affected by this illness was my father's speech. He started to stutter and had difficulties getting his words out. My father was one of the most social people I have ever met. Not being able to communicate effectively was devastating not only for my father but for those around him.

My father thrived on his connection to other people. He would happily converse with almost anybody who called and would quickly become their best friend. He had such a diverse group of clients and would drop at a dime when someone called. Watching him struggle to use the phone and then giving it up entirely was absolutely heartbreaking.

One thing that stands out from childhood was my father's fascination with James Bond. Ever since I was a child, he would tell me countless stories about Agent 007. When my father became less active, I bought him a James Bond box set. I thought he would be thrilled to watch all the James Bond movies that had been made, up to that point. When he would ask me to watch the movies with him, I was never able to enjoy them the way my father did. I would usually get bored and make up an excuse to leave before the movie was over. Although we spent time together when he was alive, opportunities I forfeited—like these precious moments—because I was "too busy," left me with a lot of regret. I also felt guilty for not doing more to care for my father on a daily basis to help him throughout his illness. Only in retrospect are we able to realize these missed opportunities.

Part of me felt conflicted because I didn't want him to feel like he was so limited by his illness. I would, therefore, pretend like it wasn't an issue on many occasions. In many ways, it was uncomfortable for both of us to discuss this because my father was a man of few words when it came to his innermost feelings. While my mother and I could converse about any topic, my father was much more guarded with his feelings and emotions. Perhaps if I had been more forthcoming about his illness, I could have been more helpful during that time.

There were many days my father would hit a new low, discovering something new that he could no longer do because of his illness. This would often spark a great deal of grief that I would want to process. If I had any plans while this was happening, I would immediately cancel them so I could go home to work with the grief in order to give it the time and space that it deserved and ultimately clear it out. Although these techniques can be used in a variety of settings, much of the inner work I did regarding my father was done when I was completely alone.

And so, on many evenings, I found myself faced with a mountain of the darkest grief I have ever known. It felt like walking into an endless and dark abyss. Having worked with stuff, I knew firsthand that it wasn't a permanent part of who I really am and could be cleared out. I was determined not to live with this heavy burden weighing me down and to use the principles and techniques I had spent so many years developing. Even though it seemed crazy, I decided to go for it! Armed with the principles and techniques we have been discussing, I dove right in.

THE ULTIMATE PARADOX

You might wonder how anyone could even begin to clear out stuff during and after the death of a parent. Why even bother to practice these techniques when faced with such a mountain of stuff? Let me shed some light on the purpose of clearing out stuff before I walk you through the process and actual techniques I used. These principles make up the theoretical framework behind this work and will illuminate what we are trying to accomplish here and how these techniques work even in the face of extreme grief.

Indefinitely holding onto grief and heavy layers of dark stuff serves no purpose other than the one you assign to it. You decide the reasons for holding onto grief, and you ultimately decide if and when you would like to be free of it. You may wallow in the grief for as long as you like but I promise you that there is always a way out. I knew that I actually had a choice to let go of the suffering and the agony. I was powerless to change the situation, but I could clear out the stuff. This means I could still find a tremendous peace and no longer be burdened by the heavy grief and dark clouds that were weighing me down. I recognized that the situation would still remain, but I no longer had to suffer the effects of holding onto the inner emotional turmoil and the suffocating clouds. This is the heart and soul of the work we have been discussing.

I no longer had to suffer the effects of holding onto the inner emotional turmoil and the suffocating clouds.

Losing a loved one is tough in every possible way. However, apart from the situation itself was the energetic pattern within me—known as grief—that is part of a broader spectrum of emotional energetic patterns we've come to know as stuff. And when it comes to stuff, we always have a choice as to how long we wish to hold on and exactly when we decide to be free of it.

This was, indeed the first thing I recognized; my father's death and the ensuing grief did not have to be forever intertwined. Separate and apart from my father's death was a completely different decision that confronted me: Do I continue to live beneath this heavy backpack that's weighing me down and hiding my joy or do I put it down?

The decision had little to do with my father and everything to do with me and my life and how I would experience my life henceforth - namely with or without a heavy backpack.

There is an incredible dichotomy at work here. Through this work, I learned to release the grief and sadness I had been carrying around with me. What's left is a sense of lightness and peace. At the same time, I was and always will be unhappy about losing my father and will miss him every day for the rest of my life. I will always feel a giant void without having my father in my life. However, I realized I no longer needed to carry a heavy backpack full of darkness, grief, and sadness. This mountain of darkness has been cleared out—automatically reconnecting me to the natural, inner happiness that resides within.

I hope you can see there is a very clear difference. It is possible to truly miss a loved one with all your heart and be forever sad about your loss without harboring all the associated stuff. You can clear it out and let it go, leaving you much lighter and connected to your inner joy. We are, thus, much more equipped to appreciate and enjoy our lives.

This chapter will walk you through the process whereby you can slowly begin putting the backpack down, unpacking just a little at a time.

PRINCIPLES FOR APPROACHING THE MOUNTAIN

When facing the mountain of grief, there were specific principles I knew to be true that gave me the courage to dive straight into the grief.

1) **Stuff can't hurt me.** No matter how scary it may appear, it is only emotional energy that can be cleared out, if desired. As we've mentioned in chapter 2, emotions might be unpleasant but are just feelings and they cannot hurt us.

2) **Stuff will keep returning until we confront it.** As we discussed in Chapter 2, emotions of this caliber and intensity need to be faced and experienced as a first step toward ultimately clearing them out. Confronting big stuff such as those surrounding the death of a loved one makes this a necessary step in the process.

3) **Stuff is only on the surface.** I knew from countless experiences that whenever I cleared out an emotion, I would always feel lighter and more peaceful. That's why I had no doubt that underneath all the grief was a lightness and freedom. Knowing that peace resided beneath the pain was my motivation.

4) **Stuff is not worth carrying the heavy load.** Having experienced life without the backpack, I felt as though continuing to live beneath such a heavy mountain of grief was no longer an option for me. I was willing to jump right in and risk everything even though it appeared that jumping right into the blackness might completely consume me.

5) **Stuff can be handled immediately.** I recognize that you can start working on stuff the moment it arises. You don't have to wait until the divorce papers have been signed or someone has passed away to begin processing the stuff you are experiencing. And this is exactly what I chose to do in that situation because so much grief was generated during my father's illness.

6) **Stuff taught me how to deal with stuff.** Although I certainly did not want to be in this situation, I knew that experiencing

the deepest, darkest grief I had ever known was a wonderful opportunity for me to put these principles to the test and would allow me the opportunity to help many other people take the same journey.

7) Stuff should clear out in any situation. I had a burning desire to know if even the heaviest kinds of darkness could clear out using this technique - if the magic worked even in the most ominous situations. There was only one way to know for sure... take the plunge and find out.

THE DETAILS

There I was, with a mountain of darkness staring me in the face. Armed with these techniques, I was ready and willing to experience, process, and do whatever it took to work through this heavy layer of grief, trusting that it could be cleared out like any other form of stuff. I started with something basic that we mentioned earlier, which is the idea of "having tea with your stuff." I had tea with the darkness and gave it the time and attention that it needed.

Rather than focusing on my day-to-day activities and ignoring all the painful emotions, I chose to focus on them each and every evening. I would allow myself to experience all the pain and sorrow without resisting it. I let it have its say without judging it.

Following The Four-Step recipe from Chapter 2, I acknowledged the existence of this seemingly horrible pain and recognized its validity. I allowed myself to experience the full palette of emotions no matter how dark they appeared to be. Some of this grief was frightening. It was so dark I was afraid it would swallow me up, never to be seen or heard from again. Nevertheless, I chose to move right into it.

After practicing this work for so many years, I knew that it couldn't hurt me. Was it extremely unpleasant? Absolutely. But I knew that I wanted to work through this so I could get back in touch with the real me. I allowed myself to respond to the stuff without judging my reaction. There were times I would cry, sob, or even scream. I took as much time as I needed. Sometimes the grief and sorrow would be so intense that it caused me to fall to the floor with sorrow—tears flooding through me. I knew that these emotions couldn't hurt me; it's just emotional energy that needed to be expressed, embraced, and ultimately released.

I continually moved into those parts of myself that were suffering since I knew that ignoring or resisting the hurt would only cause the pain to persist. I tried to maintain compassion and love for the hurt and pain that dwelled within me. I maintained the perspective that all the stuff—the emotional patterns—can be cleared out.

After giving myself enough time to cry, scream, and sit with the grief, at some point during this process I would gauge when I was ready to let go. This usually happened after I gave a certain amount of attention and compassion to my emotions and allowed myself to fully experience them. It was a visceral feeling, no longer wanting to carry this burden with me.

This is a very important concept that we introduced in Chapter 2 and it warrants repeating here:

When you allow your stuff to surface, it's important to pay attention to how you are feeling towards it.

At some point you will sense a shift, letting you know that you are ready to let go. It's easy to know when you have reached this point. All you need to do is ask yourself if you feel ready to let go. If you are ready, the question will sound like a welcome relief because you will desire to be free of the burden you are carrying. On the other hand, if you aren't ready to let go, the idea will sound preposterous and you will strongly resist letting go. Continue to sit with the stuff until you're ready to let go. Yes, even in this situation, you don't have to walk around with darkness as your constant companion.

And so at this point, I would write a heartfelt letter asking to have the stuff cleared out. Each night before I went to sleep, I would write a letter to God, asking to have all the grief cleared out while I slept and to be worked on all through the night. Remember that it's the sincere, heartfelt intention that is really important here. God will do all the rest and take you out of the darkness.

Nearly every morning I would wake up clear as a bell as if all the grief, sadness, and darkness had been lifted off of me—leaving me clear, light, and peaceful. I felt completely cleaned out, and all that remained was a feeling of happiness and contentment. It was astounding to awaken each morning feeling so wonderful after experiencing such heavy and intense stuff the previous night. Each night, I would peel whatever layer of the onion happened to present itself that day. And each morning I would awaken feeling clear and light.

Initially, the grief was intense when triggered, but that severity gradually decreased as though the volume was being turned down. Each time it did return, it was quieter and less menacing. And there were longer and longer periods of time before the next layer of stuff would surface, leaving me with longer and longer periods of peace and calm in between.

Clearing out the stuff each night helped to do two things:

1. It allowed me to experience a wonderful respite from the heavy burden of grief and sadness each day, thereby allowing me to connect with my father much more effectively while he lived. During this time, I was able to breathe and relax as well.

2. As I continued to clear out the grief each day, I noticed that it became lighter and lighter each time it returned. I would repeat the process, allowing me to peel the onion, one layer at a time.

I continued this process throughout my father's illness, which went on for several years. I have been practicing this work for 15 years and it has never failed me. I believe that if you have a true desire to practice the seven steps with a willingness to let go, you will experience magical shifts in your life.

ONE CHOICE TO MAKE

Losing a loved one is a terrible thing that will leave you forever missing the person, and there is obviously nothing you can do to change the situation. This kind of loss is like being wrongfully punched in the nose by life. You might not feel like seeking treatment for the broken nose since you are so opposed to this terrible situation. However, you *can* alleviate the pain caused by your broken nose. It won't change the situation, but it will relieve the tremendous amount of ongoing suffering and grief. You can begin to feel light again, even amid the darkness. You can repair the broken nose and rid yourself of the unnecessary hurt and suffering. You can process the grief and let it go.

If you have suffered the loss of a loved one, you have a simple yet significant choice to make. You do not have to continuously live with emotional pain. Using the techniques outlined in this book, you can free yourself from years and years of darkness. It doesn't matter how long you have lived with your stuff, using this technique is your way out. While there is nothing you can do to change the situation, the magic steps will change the way you experience the rest of your life and will dramatically alter the way you feel and experience life henceforth.

So, which do you choose? Do you want to indefinitely carry the anguish and grief with you? Or would you rather put the backpack down allowing yourself to access the happiness hiding underneath? This pivotal choice can profoundly change the way you will experience your future. You will forever miss your loved one, but you will not be bogged down beneath the stuff. When the stuff is cleared out, it allows you to breathe again… play again… laugh again… and love again.

If you're ready to muster up the courage and strength to ask to have it cleared out for you, then you are ready to begin an incredible journey that will restore your happiness and peace.

IN A NUTSHELL

Despite hearing my story and explicit instructions, people often tell me that it still perplexes them to follow the specific steps in clearing out grief. Even though we have been explicitly discussing the seven magic steps, sometimes it is difficult to integrate them into a specific plan of action. The following synopsis gets right to the point to sum up the specific actions that will enable you to work through the grieving process.

If you have lost a loved one, take the time to sit with the grief and allow it to express itself. Look it right in the eye. This might be unthinkable to you. Do it anyway. I promise that it can't hurt you. It's just stuff. It's not pleasant. Just know that the rewards will far outweigh the temporary discomfort.

Let yourself confront the pain. If you feel the need, talk about your feelings for as long as you like. Speak to your friends and family about your emotions. And always remember to have compassion for your emotions. Don't judge them as good or bad. No emotions are off limits. If you feel anger, hate, sadness, grief, or anything else, spend time with those feelings as you allow them to surface. Spend time each day just being with the grief and the pain and allow it to express. Cry, yell, laugh, or sob. See the emotions as small children or pets—embrace them and give them compassion and love. See yourself hugging them and sending them love for as long as you need.

When you are ready, ask or write a heartfelt letter each night before going to sleep to have this grief cleared out. I personally addressed these letters to God, but as you know from Chapter 2, you may substitute your preferred language. In my writing, I expressed my heartfelt desire to have God work on me while I sleep and asked to have the grief cleared out. I invited God to come join in the grief and help it to go away. When you write your letter, be sure to mention that you want to wake up feeling clear, light, and even joyous. If you ask this from your heart each night and would prefer happiness over the grief, it will begin to clear. There will often be a noticeable and dramatic difference each morning.

If more grief arises the next day, take time to be with that grief as well. Remember that whatever you choose to confront can't hurt you, just like walking up to the Wizard. This will allow the grief, pain, and sorrow to begin to loosen its grip on you. If you couple this process with writing sincere letters or making requests each evening to have the stuff cleared out while you sleep, the results can be astounding.

The bottom line:

Do not despair, no matter what kind of suffering you are experiencing. Even the darkness and grief of losing a loved one can be processed, experienced, and ultimately released in a healthy manner. I found it nothing less than miraculous when clearing out stuff from losing my father.

If you are willing to follow the magic steps and sincerely desire to clear out the stuff, it will work. Every. Single. Time.

―――――――――

THE PASSING STORM: A BEAUTIFUL ANALOGY OF HOW TO PROCESS GRIEF

When grief and hurt arise, you can view it as a passing storm in the night. You can allow the grief to soak you… and then ask to have it cleared out… allowing it to pass right over you. You don't have to make your home there. It's just a passing storm.

I saw the grief that arose each day as a passing storm. I gave it the attention that it deserved spending time getting wet and processing each storm. I knew the storm would ultimately pass, so I asked for it to clear out and move on. I didn't choose to indefinitely dwell within the storm.

A passing storm deserves your attention. However, it doesn't have to completely overtake you and become your identity. It's just a passing storm— nothing more and nothing less.

Each day when the grief would arise, I would allow it to surface, speak, and have its say. It spoke of tremendous pain at losing my precious dad, and how dark things appeared to be without him. Continuing to live without him seemed like a dark and bleak future; an inescapable void.

Yet I knew that this, too, could be processed and cleared out. The situation wasn't going to change, but the dark storm clouds could be processed and cleared out. I didn't have to take up a permanent dwelling amidst the storm because the storm doesn't have to grow to define you. It's just "stuff" that can be processed, learned from, and let go.

You need only to remember that you are not the stuff and you can begin to slowly put the backpack down, a little bit at a time. If you have the sincere desire to let go and the courage to look your stuff in the eye and follow these techniques, you will succeed.

In truth, the stuff was not bad. It was just "stuff" that arose and needed to be looked at, loved, experienced, and released. It won't change how much I miss my father or the situation itself. However, putting the stuff down has given me a tremendous amount of peace and joy to continue to live my life.

Nobody says that you have to indefinitely carry around a mountain of grief, anger, and sadness, as it can be cleared out, even amidst the incredible loss of losing a loved one. Only you can decide when the time is right to release yourself from this heavy burden.

Your life will never be the same after reading this far. You have a way out. You now know that there is a choice about how you wish to experience loss. You now have mighty tools that can help you get through any situation. You don't have to endlessly live with sadness and grief as you have finally found a doorway that leads to peace.

I wish you peace and joy on your journey through the darkness.

CHAPTER 5 SUMMARY

Losing a loved one is never easy, but you can still clear out the emotional pain—the stuff—despite the circumstances.

Grief can gradually clear out in layers. Don't be afraid to dive in and completely experience it, talk about it, and express it.

When you're ready, write nightly letters asking to have the stuff cleared out while you sleep. It will return lighter each time. You might also experience periods of peace before it returns.

Even though it won't change the situation, it will completely change your entire life experience.

By removing the dark and heavy clouds, you will allow yourself to breathe again and experience peace as you move forward.

6

The Many Faces of Stuff

BEING VICTIMIZED

One evening, my wife and I arrived home to discover someone had burglarized our house. Clothes and other objects were strewn all over the place as though someone had quickly rummaged through all of our belongings. You can imagine the flood of thoughts and emotions that came over me as I walked into my home. These three were the strongest for me:

Anger. An anger erupted in me at the thought of a stranger forcing their way into my home and sifting through my personal things. Part of me wanted to immediately find the perpetrators and bring and bring them to justice. I felt that in order for me to find peace and get past this incident, the perpetrator needed to face justice immediately.

Fear. It was terrifying to know that someone broke into my home and could do it again. Each day following the incident, I would enter the house afraid to find out whether there had been another burglary. **The "ick factor."** There was an icky factor that accompanied this experience. I felt creeped out that someone had violated us, and the feeling continued to linger each time I returned home. I felt uneasy about the whole thing and was no longer at peace in my own home. On the one hand, I knew that all of this stuff could be cleared out and I didn't want to hang on any longer than necessary. On the other hand, this had really done a number on me. I knew I would need to spend some time confronting and experiencing these extremely uncomfortable emotions before I could do any meaningful clearing. It was apparent that I wasn't ready to let go of any of this and was, therefore, not ready to use the magic. Remember that we need to allow heavy stuff to surface so it can be confronted and experienced before it can be cleared out. And that was definitely the case in this situation!

I truly wanted to give these heavy emotions the time and space they needed and deserved, so I made a conscious effort to experience the stuff. I allowed myself to swim in all the emotions I was feeling. I faced the anger that I had and invited it into my awareness. I also confronted the hatred I felt toward the perpetrators along with my own human need to punish them. I permitted myself to revel in these emotions for as long as it felt appropriate. At times, I would just sit there with all the feelings bubbling around me—yelling, screaming, and even speaking to the perpetrators in my mind and telling them how I felt.

The key was to not suppress any of these feelings and allow all of them to be present with me. The more uncomfortable the emotion, the more I moved into it and allowed myself to experience it. I didn't judge it as good or bad. I allowed myself to feel and accept it.

I also made sure to directly confront the icky feeling, keeping in mind that the ultimate goal was to let this stuff go. I knew I didn't want to carry it around with me for a long period of time. Again, I sat with the emotions and gave them the space they deserved. I resisted nothing.

It may be tempting to avoid these emotions since they aren't exactly comfortable. But I wanted to look them straight in the eye and embrace them in order to hasten my desire and readiness to make a sincere request to have it all cleared out. I wanted to use the magic;

I just wasn't quite ready yet. So, I immersed myself in these emotions for several days because I knew the only way to bring this about was to look at these emotions, feel them, and talk about them. Three days is all it took.

What's important to note here, you cannot artificially rush this process. Initially, I wanted to clear out all the stuff right there on the spot. However, I still had too much anger and other forms of stuff to process. Therefore, I had to take a few days and give it the attention it deserved. Once I did this, there was a moment I became aware I was ready to let go. It felt like an inner recognition that I don't have to live with this pain any longer and was truly ready to let go. My desire for peace outweighed my desire to hang onto the stuff any longer. And it wasn't forced. I had a true willingness to let go of the stuff and finally be free of it.

When you're ready to let go, you will know it in your heart. In these cases, there is no need to formally ask yourself if you are willing to let go as we discussed in Chapter 2. In this instance, I knew with certainty that I no longer needed to hold onto the stuff any longer and could immediately write the letter. I was extremely receptive to the idea and couldn't wait.

In truth, I wasn't motivated by the idea of being kind to the people who burglarized me. Rather, I no longer wanted to be imprisoned by the heavy load I had been carrying around for those several days. It was incredibly exhausting being consumed by this burden, and I suddenly recognized I had no further need to experience or hold onto this stuff any longer.

After experiencing the sincere desire to let go, I immediately wrote a heartfelt letter asking to have the stuff cleared out. The stuff began clearing out even before I started writing the letter. My desire to let go, coupled with my intention to have the stuff cleared out, immedi lately began clearing out as I set the intention.

In the letter, I clearly stated that I had no more need for the anger, fear, and creepiness, and I was ready to let it go. I asked to have all of it cleared out, and by that point, a lot of it had. It continued to lift off me as I typed. One by one, I could feel the anger, fear, and icky feelings clearing off of me. It felt like walking out of a dungeon and into the sunlight. One minute, all of this stuff was suffocating me. A few minutes later, I felt light as a feather and back to my old self. It felt so good to breathe again.

My house felt like my home again. I was no longer seeing it through the prism of fear and anger. The idea of being burglarized no longer had the negative charge surrounding it. It felt like such a tremendous burden had been lifted off of me and, indeed it had.

Releasing the anger, fear, and icky feelings in no way means I am happy about what happened or that I condone the perpetrator's behavior. Making the choice to let go of those emotions does not change the fact that the burglary had occurred. What did I gain from letting go? The ability to feel peace again.

A SURPRISING THING HAPPENED

Sometimes, clearing out the stuff can have surprising results. An interesting thing happened after I successfully cleared out the stuff surrounding the burglary. I actually began having compassion for the burglar. Once I was no longer seeing the crime through a veil of hate, anger, and fear, things looked very different. It was much easier for me to see what terrible shape they must have been in, risking prison time for what amounted to just a pittance in stolen goods.

Life looks quite different when it is not being seen through the prism of our stuff. Suddenly, we can see things more clearly. I wasn't trying to have compassion for the burglars(s), but in the absence of the stuff, I began seeing them through my heart.

THERE IS NO NEED TO WAIT

Forgiveness is not saying it's okay that someone committed a crime against you. It's not okay! What they did was wrong, and they deserve whatever punishment befalls them for it. If someone hurts you or a loved one, it is obviously NOT okay. However, letting go of the stuff surrounding the crime—the anger, hurt, sadness, and grief—is for YOU. It allows you to return to your peace of mind immediately.

You don't need to wait until the person is jailed or punished in other ways. You can let go of the stuff the moment you are ready to feel better. Often when people are victimized, they tend to hold onto their stuff, only allowing themselves to let go if there is some kind of perceived justice. This can take the form of the person being caught, the stolen item being returned, etc.

These are only arbitrary conditions that we decide must be present before we are willing to let go of our stuff. We have the choice to let go as soon as we are ready to face our stuff and work through it using the magic steps.

In many cases, even after some perceived justice occurs, people will often continue to harbor stuff in various forms that will continue to rob them of their peace long after the incident is over. Nothing has to change externally for us to reach this point other than a willingness and a desire for peace over whatever the perceived benefits are of continuing to hold onto this stuff. As I've stated before, if we have the desire to look at our stuff and experience it, it will lead to a desire to let it go.

It is only unexperienced stuff that tempts us to continue to hold on. Once you have given the stuff a voice, expressed it, seen it, and spoken about it for the purpose of healing it, you will no longer desire to hold on indefinitely and will quickly lose interest in it. Not because it's the right thing to do but for the simple reason that it is destroying your peace of mind! Peace offers so much more than anything the stuff ever could.

I still have to contend with the burglary such as continuing to file the necessary paperwork and replacing the lost items. But catching the perpetrators will add nothing to the peace I feel. I might be interested in finding out more details if they are caught, but I will not feel additional peace because I have let go of the only true obstacles to peace: the stuff.

VICTIM VS. STUFF

Throughout the process, I refused to see myself as a victim. Playing the victim means we are creating an identity out of the stuff that has arisen. We become an angry or resentful person by incorporating the stuff into our sense of self. Instead, I chose to see it as stuff and not define myself by it. It was only stuff—nothing more, nothing less. I didn't have to carry it with me and embrace it as a new part of myself. The decision I faced was to either create a new identity where I carried all of this new stuff with me or to let go and have my peace restored. It wound up being an easy decision. I chose to recognize these emotions as stuff that can be cleared out and let go, which made me feel like a million bucks because the relief was so deep, transformative, and significant.

Never give up on peace. It can always be found hiding just beneath the surface of your stuff.

GUILT AND SELF-JUDGMENT

All guilt begins and ends with you. You are the only person who can make yourself feel guilty. You are also the only one who can free yourself of guilt. You decide the moment of your release.

When we feel guilty, we often think the cause of the guilt is from something in the outside world—a teacher, parent, God, or a life situation. The key is to recognize that guilt is simply another form of stuff that gets triggered from within and can be cleared out at any time. In an instant, you can begin working with the guilt and clearing it out.

Many of us have been conditioned by parents and teachers to feel guilty about everything—from the foods we eat and the clothes we wear to the religious rituals we practice. Oftentimes, there is an abundance of guilt lying dormant within each of us that was conditioned from childhood. When it is triggered, we have the opportunity to clear it out like all of the other kinds of stuff we have been discussing.

Guilt can serve a great purpose by using it constructively to reevaluate your actions. Suppose you feel guilty about not being more helpful when a friend really needed you. Obviously, the emotion of guilt can be used to help you reassess your actions. You can then think about how you wish you had reacted and note those changes for the future. However, there is no point in continuing to indefinitely hold onto the guilt. This is just another form of stuff that has been triggered, and you now have the opportunity to heal this guilt. Holding onto it further serves no purpose other than continuing to perpetuate this guilty feeling. Like any other form of stuff, it can be released whenever you are ready.

All you are doing when you choose to hold onto guilt is continually punish yourself. Only you can decide if and when this self-flagellation stops!

HOW IS GUILT CREATED IN THE FIRST PLACE?

We can create guilt in two primary ways:

1) **An event can trigger past guilt and bring it back to the surface.** Suppose eating sweets and junk food makes you feel guilty. Perhaps as a child, you learned "dessert is bad" and so you naturally felt guilty every time you ate it. If you've never cleared out and released the guilt, it will remain dormant in you waiting for that triggering event so it can resurface.

2) **Guilt can originate WITHIN YOU, courtesy of the incessant mental chatter in our head.** Suppose you read an article about sweets, and every time you eat them you tell yourself you're terrible for eating sweets or that they will make you fat. Now you are generating these emotions in real time from your own thoughts inside your head.

Either way, however the guilt manifested, you have a tremendous opportunity to correctly identify the guilt as "stuff" and actually heal it.

Guilt can plague every waking moment of someone's life and consume them. I have seen this happen many times, especially when people make a mistake and can never seem to forgive themselves. Remember, forgiving yourself is merely letting go of the energy of guilt and allowing yourself to let it go. You are not condoning the actions you might have taken to trigger the guilt. In the case of eating sweets, you can use the guilt to make dietary changes, but there is no constructive reason to live with guilt about your food choices for the rest of your life. You can make informed decisions about what foods to eat without suffering the effects of constantly feeling guilty!

Lauren and Princess

Suppose you had a friend named Lauren who has a dog named Princess. Princess becomes very ill. The vet gives her numerous treatment options, leaving the decision ultimately in Lauren's hands. After much deliberation, Lauren decides which treatment option sounds the best. They administer the treatment and, unfortunately, Princess passes away.

This situation will naturally trigger a tremendous amount of guilt within Lauren, and she might be tough on herself. She might tell herself *You killed Princess,* or *It's all your fault Princess is gone!*

Not to minimize the terrible loss suffered here, however, there is no reason for Lauren to walk around being burdened with guilt. It can be cleared out like any other form of stuff. In this case, Lauren must recognize the source of the guilt lies within her. She must see the guilt as stuff, an energetic pattern that has arisen in response to Princess's death. In any moment, she can decide to let go of this stuff called guilt and return to peace.

Remember "all guilt begins and ends with you." You can decide when to allow yourself to go free. Nobody is forcing you to walk around feeling this way! You have a choice. You always have a choice. Use the seven steps and move on with your life. As with any other form of stuff, the steps will always work magic.

By now, you are hopefully learning the routine and becoming more comfortable with the magic steps. As you know, sometimes a simple letter will do the trick. And if you're not yet ready for the letter, you can step into the feelings and allow yourself to experience them—even if it means talking about them with friends and family. When it feels appropriate, begin writing the letter or making the request. It might clear out immediately, or over time in layers, as intense stuff often does. This might require repeating this process until all the guilt is cleared out. But once you clear it, you are now forever free from the guilt you picked up in childhood or elsewhere. And each morning you will feel lighter as the guilt continues to diminish.

Some people spend years riddled with guilt, and their lives can become completely stagnant because of it. The issues surrounding this guilt can sometimes be quite intense. They should have been kinder to their parents when they had the chance, or they could have prevented their divorce if they would have worked harder. Whatever happened has happened, and you cannot change it. However, you can certainly learn much from the past as you move forward. The bottom line is there is no reason to endlessly tote around guilt other than the reason that you choose to tell yourself.

Ultimately, you have a choice about letting go of the energetic pattern of guilt in the same manner you have a choice to let go of anger, grief, and other forms of stuff we have been discussing in this book.

My Dad

As I mentioned in Chapter 5, after my father passed away, one emotion I had to deal with was guilt. I felt guilty that I hadn't done certain things while my father was ill. I regretted not doing certain things while he was healthy. One thing I mentioned was guilt for not spending more time with my father after his illness began.

The first thing I did was to recognize the source of the guilt. The source was inside me which meant I would have to confront the stuff lying dormant with me if I wanted it to clear. I went to work confronting the guilt, allowing it to wash over me. It was uncomfortable and unpleasant. So I spent considerable time facing the guilt and also talking about it.

When I was ready to let go and able to wholeheartedly ask to have the guilt cleared out, I started writing my letters and petitioned from my heart. Like other forms of stuff we have been discussing, it cleared out.

RELIGIOUS GUILT

One destructive way that guilt can manifest is in association with one's particular faith or religious beliefs. We are by no means evaluating the truth or merits of any particular religious faith, but rather how the destructive emotion called guilt can operate within this context.

With religion, guilt can also be used as a constructive emotion, allowing us to reevaluate our actions. However, there is no reason to continue to hold onto the guilt indefinitely, sometimes creating a lifetime of suffering.

For example, suppose someone decides to leave their particular faith or become more or less religiously observant than the rest of their family. This decision need not be accompanied by a lifetime of guilt. Like any other emotion, we can clear the guilt and let go. I have known people who have had their entire lives consumed by religious guilt. They grew up believing certain things and were told about the horrible consequences of not following in the footsteps of their parents, teachers, or clergy. This guilt can stay with someone for a lifetime.

In any and all of these cases, the guilt does not have to become a lifetime companion. You now hold the keys to releasing this guilt if you so desire. Most importantly, you must be willing to face the guilt and have a desire to let go. The seven magic steps can successfully release you from a lifetime of guilt if you are willing to work with them.

SEXUAL GUILT

Similarly, there are countless people riddled with sexual guilt and fear. Some people are raised with lots of shame regarding sex. In many cases, our parents themselves are not comfortable with sex, and this discomfort gets passed onto their children. Sometimes these children are so affected that they cannot have healthy sexual relationships as adults due to their deep-rooted guilt. Whatever the reason, we can clear the guilt surrounding the sexual issues using the magic steps to restore our peace.

You are the only one who can free yourself of guilt as it all originates from within.

You decide the moment of your release.

You wait only for yourself.

SELF-ACCEPTANCE

Did you know that you can clear out your self-image? Many of us have an underlying negative self-image of who we are. Even though we are perfection and greatness, the thing that prevents us from experiencing this and knowing who we truly are is the stuff that gets in the way. The stuff is insecurity, self-doubt, self-loathing, guilt, and all the other negative stuff that we carry around with us.

We create these feelings in response to the things we are told by our parents and teachers, giving rise to countless amounts of shame and self-doubt among other things. And these emotions, in turn, influence our thoughts, giving rise to all kinds of negative self-talk. This causes even more feelings of self-loathing and self-doubt creating a vicious cycle that prevents us from experiencing our true essence.

Once these negative emotions are created, people will often spend a lifetime trying to use their accomplishments to mask all these underlying feelings of inadequacy. But these underlying feelings are nothing more than stuff that can be cleared out, just like any other kind of stuff we have been discussing.

Your stuff masks your natural confidence that lives just beneath the surface of all this negative stuff. Clearing out a negative self-image requires a desire to clear out all these false insecurities and other forms of stuff that is not the real you. This will automatically reveal your true self underneath.

How do you know if something is not the real you? The answer is simple. It doesn't feel good!

Even if you feel like a loser, you can clear that pattern and emotion revealing the true greatness that lies underneath. If you feel unworthy, you must challenge this emotion as it, too, can be cleared out to reveal the truth underneath. In other words, you must be willing to challenge all the beliefs and feelings you have had about yourself until now and start to see yourself as something great. If a belief doesn't feel good, you can bet it is stuff that can be cleared out.

All the negativity, self-hatred, and feelings of unworthiness can be cleared out. Each of us carries around countless amounts of stuff regarding our self-image—all of which can be cleared out because it's not the real you. Stop insisting you know who and what you are. Let your true self reveal itself to you. You have to stop defining yourself in order to see who you truly are. In the absence of your stuff, your true self can shine forth.

When you are willing to question every last piece of stuff regarding your identity, the person you truly are has the space to come forth. Stop believing in your stuff and start believing in yourself.

One of the greatest shifts in the lifetime of a human being is recognizing who you truly are underneath all your stuff. This opens the door to true self-acceptance. At our core, many of us believe that we are not lovable, worthy, or good. Some of us even believe that we are downright evil. However, underneath all these false beliefs lies the feeling of perfection that is the real you. This is the natural feeling that manifests when you clear out the stuff that has been hiding and obscuring this truth from you.

The philosophy of this book is that who and what we are can never change. Our soul is greatness and perfection. The only thing that can change is the false identity we create when we identify with our stuff. Don't take my word for it. This is something you can feel and know directly when you begin clearing out the stuff that is obscuring your true self-image.

I'll never forget watching an interview of an extremely successful singer on television. She mentioned that despite having millions of adoring fans and having achieved a high level of success, she still did not feel good about herself.

Until you experience and touch your true nature, no amount of external success will totally mask underlying feelings of insecurity. Some of the most successful people on the planet have admitted how they still struggle with their negative self-image. Some of the most talented people have discussed how much underlying insecurity they have.

The only way to know and experience a true, deep, and abiding sense of self-worth is to know and feel who you truly are. And the only way to do this is by clearing out all the layers upon layers of stuff that obscure it, preventing you from feeling how great your true self really feels. We can clear self-doubt, self-loathing, self-guilt, and self-hatred, along with all of the other forms of stuff because they are all equally false.

THE BASIS OF SELF-ACCEPTANCE

One of the most incredible realizations is that there is nothing we can do to makes ourselves feel worthy or great. We are great by virtue of who and what we are inside. This is the true basis for self-acceptance and self-worth.

Your worth comes from who and what you are—that true essence inside each of us—and not from what you do. There is nothing you can do to make you feel truly worthy until you are able to come into contact with your true nature.

How to Start

There are two simple ways to help clear out your current self-image.

First, you can start questioning every feeling and belief you have ever had about yourself. Look each one of them straight in the eye and subject it to the same process we have described for the different types of stuff you might encounter. Walk directly into it, look at it, and feel it. You might also wish to speak about it. Be loving and compassionate to those parts of yourself that feel unworthy.

Next, come up with a few statements about yourself that are incredible. If you don't believe the statements because they sound too good to be true, then they are perfect! It will help trigger all the insecurities and self-doubt regarding your self-image and bring it to the surface. You can then clear it out.

Or you can use my statement, which I believe is true about our essence:

"You are the greatest thing that has ever lived. You are the most awesome, the most incredible, the most wondrous, and the most special. You are the worthiest. You are the most precious. And you are a part of the Universe/the Creator/God itself."

Any resistance that comes up in response to these statements can be continuously cleared out. It makes no difference if you believe it or not. Just keep telling yourself this and keep clearing out any stuff that arises in response to it. As you keep writing letters and asking to clear out any stuff that is associated with your self-image and continue to practice the magic, you will begin to come in contact with your true self. All you have to do is be willing to sincerely ask to have your stuff cleared out and confront it once and for all. Then sit back and watch the magic unfold.

SADNESS

Sometimes, the clouds are so dark it looks like night. Remember, the sun is still shining beneath the clouds. No matter how dark things get, the stuff can always be cleared out.

Sadness is often an intense form of stuff that makes it easy to forget the seven steps. People experiencing tremendous sadness will often tell me they don't know where to start. Since sadness can sometimes be stifling, it can help to walk through the techniques one step at a time.

If you are suffering from sadness, I want you to walk right into it. That's right. I know it sounds crazy but allow the sadness to wash over you and walk right into it.

While you are inside, I want you to remember that this is just another form of stuff and therefore cannot hurt you no matter how bad it might feel. Allow it to speak to you. Sit with it and "have tea," allowing yourself to feel it and experience it. Talk about it with a friend or licensed counselor. Have compassion for it.

You might feel like crying. You might feel like screaming at the top of your lungs. You might want to talk to a friend or counselor and express everything you are feeling at this moment. Those are all perfectly okay.

Remember that facing, confronting, and speaking about stuff is often a prerequisite for its demise. It spells the beginning of the end when it comes to stuff.

Sadness often has to be cleared out in layers. While you work with the seven steps, remember to ask yourself throughout this process if you are ready to let go. If the idea feels like a welcome relief and something that feels good and energizing, go for it!

Next, I want you to summon the courage to write a letter. Remember the only requirement is that it comes from the heart and that you are willing to let go. Ask from the bottom of your heart to have the stuff cleared out. State that you are now ready to let it go and need help clearing it out. You can call it "sadness," "stuff," "despair," or any other term you choose. The exact words are not important here. What's important is the intention and desire to have the stuff cleared out for you.

Make sure you write a letter every night before you go to sleep, asking to be worked on throughout the night and to have all of this darkness lifted off and cleared out. If you ask from your heart and insist that the stuff be cleared out AND you are truly willing to let go, it will start to shift. Each morning you should wake up a little bit lighter. When more stuff arises, start the process all over again. The next morning you will awaken yet again feeling even lighter and more connected to yourself.

You can even write a letter upon awakening, asking to have the sadness cleared out throughout the day and giving thanks for the clearing that has taken place so far. Continue peeling off layer after layer of stuff. It will continue to get lighter and lighter, and you might experience periods of happiness before the stuff returns. And each time it returns, the stuff will be lighter and less smothering. You are experiencing more sunlight as the clouds continue to dissipate. The results from this simple regimen can move mountains, and I have seen people completely change in a matter of days.

Turn everything over to God/The Universe/the Creator or wherever you are making your request. Open the doors and windows and allow the help to enter.

DEPRESSION

Depression can stem from multiple sources, including but not limited to a neurotransmitter imbalance, trauma, or situational changes. Only a licensed healthcare professional can make that determination.

Some forms of counseling can involve working with the emotions and confronting them in order to heal them. The techniques in this book share a similar goal and can help significantly towards that end.

First and foremost, remember not to shy away from the sadness. Although it may feel unpleasant and uncomfortable, sadness cannot hurt you. As we covered earlier, sadness is another form of stuff. Always try to summon the courage to walk into the sadness and experience the emotions. It's important to not personalize the emotions or allow them to take up residence within your house.

In my experience, when the intense sadness and grief concerning my father surfaced, I was determined to dive head first into the darkness. Even though it was daunting, I refused to see the emotions as a permanent part of who I am. I saw them as a form of stuff I needed to spend time with and acknowledge before I could let them go. With this determination, I was able to successfully use all the techniques I outlined in the chapter on grief and throughout this book.

Had I chosen to embrace the grief as a part of myself and allowed it to take up permanent residence within me, this might have ended quite differently. Utilizing the seven steps has enabled me to move forward and put down the heavy backpack.

Sometimes we are in need of help to allow these feelings to surface. We can feel overwhelmed when they do. This is another instance where a licensed professional can make all the difference by helping us confront the stuff in order to let it go and ultimately write that letter.

Whatever you do, try not to keep these emotions locked away in a room. Open the door and allow the sunlight to come shining in.

FEAR

Fear is a phony. It is nothing more than an illusion trying to convince you it is real. Don't believe it! It might look terrifying but it's just a scary set on a Hollywood movie. Underneath the scary illusion is just another form of stuff. And how do you reveal the true nature of an illusion? You have to walk right up to it while keeping in mind it is just stuff that can be cleared out.

Fear is not who we are. Like all stuff, it is a case of mistaken identity. Fear is stuff we've falsely identified as real and a part of ourselves. When we believe the fear is real, we preclude any possibility of healing it. Now that it is seen as real, how can you clear it out? In order to heal and clear out the fear, you have to recognize it as stuff.

CLEARING OUT FEAR IN A FEW PARAGRAPHS

By now you know the drill for clearing out stuff. Even with this knowledge, I've often had people tell me "but this situation is different because I have so much fear associated with it." Therefore, it can be helpful to have the steps spelled out for you.

Remember, fear is just another form of stuff. One key in successfully dealing with fear is to keep confronting it. Look at it directly and it will change right before your eyes. The more you look, feel, talk about, and give attention to the fear, the less power it has over you. The more you avoid talking about it, experiencing it, and confronting it, the more power it has over you.

Don't be scared to walk right into the fear. While you're experiencing the fear, take deep breaths. Don't resist it. Don't fight it. Allow it to be there. Acknowledge its right to exist.

Sometimes people have lots of fear which can cause everything they see and do to continually trigger this fear. Until you clear out the fear at its source, it will activate in a never-ending cycle where even simple activities become very fearful.

It's important to point out we are not talking about natural real time fear that is generated by your body in response to danger, which is a fight-or-flight reaction. Your body naturally generates the fear in response to various situations for survival. What we are talking about is harboring self-generated fears that can persist sometimes for many years.

Perhaps we are overly anxious about something that hasn't happened and has persisted in generating fear on a daily basis. We can clear out this kind of fear. Though we cannot change the situation, we can clear out the fear—restoring our peace of mind. We are now better equipped to deal with the situation that triggered the fear in the first place.

By now you know the routine, but let's quickly recap:

Like every other form of stuff: confront the fear, allow yourself to feel it, talk about it, and have true compassion for it.

When you feel ready, write a heartfelt letter or make a request asking to have the fear cleared out. Be especially careful to write this letter before bedtime, asking to be worked on throughout the night, having the fear cleared out and waking up feeling clear, happy, and joyous.

Suppose you have an intense fear about your finances. Perhaps you are unsure about the future of your current job and are constantly fearful about your current financial situation. Whatever the situation, apart from the monetary situation you find yourself in is the stuff that is producing the emotion of fear. And the good news is we can clear the stuff—leaving a feeling peace. Obviously, your financial situation will remain the same and you will have to deal with it. But you won't be carrying around the stuff called fear and you will actually feel lighter even though the situation persists.

The bottom line:

You do not have to live needlessly with fear. You always hold the key to release yourself from all fears using the techniques we have been discussing. Only you can decide when your moment of release will come.

―――――――

ANGER, FORGIVENESS, AND THE ULTIMATE PARADOX

Forgiveness has little to do with the other person. You don't forgive for the other person's sake. You forgive so you can let go of all the poison you are carrying around, the stuff which is robbing you of your peace of mind. You can let the stuff clear out in order to restore your peace.

Forgiveness is not about overlooking another person's actions. If someone is mean-spirited and mistreats you by verbally, emotionally, or physically abusing you, you obviously don't have to pretend that everything is okay and continue to associate with that person. You can clear out the anger and wish the person well while simultaneously having no future dealings.

Perhaps you believe the person is troubled and needs help. Now that you are no longer holding onto the stuff, you can still access peace even though the other person's actions were harmful. You can choose peace by letting go of your stuff. This is a personal decision you make for YOURSELF. It is self-motivated because it will return you to the peace you deserve.

QUICK SUMMARY OF THE PROCESS: THE ANGER PURGE

Below, I summarize the process of clearing out anger with highlights that relate specifically to anger.

The first pivotal thing to do is to remain cognizant of the anger without being swept up in this intense and powerful emotion. Feel and observe the anger without being consumed by it. As powerful and loud as anger can be, you can clear it out just like any other emotion.

Make a request or write a letter right off the bat, asking to have the anger cleared out. As noted in Chapter 4, sometimes letter writing can have instant results. I have experienced successfully clearing out tremendous amounts of anger just moments after the anger arose simply by writing a letter. It has floored me when this has happened! However, as we've mentioned throughout this book, you might need to do a few things first before you are willing to sincerely write a letter asking to have the anger cleared out.

We've talked about how, in some cases, the magic of this technique will only work after you have experienced the stuff first. You may need to yell or scream, hit a pillow, or speak to someone and express your anger. Most times, intense anger needs to be experienced, expressed, or spoken about before we are willing to pray or write a letter asking to have it cleared out. This will often bring us to a place where we are ready and willing to let go.

Keep in mind that your purpose in experiencing, expressing, and speaking about the anger is to release it rather than to fuel more of it. Anger is just an energy that needs to be expressed. Otherwise the anger will just go back to sleep and awaken again in response to the next person or event that brings it back to the surface.

Periodically ask yourself if you would be willing to let go of the anger. If you feel resistance and angry at this idea, you aren't ready to let go and need to continue talking and experiencing your feelings.

However, if you are open to the idea and it feels like a welcomed relief, you are in a much better position to write the letters. Start writing, especially before bedtime, asking to have the anger cleared out. It might clear out in layers, each time returning with less intensity. The question always comes down to this: Would you prefer to have the anger or the peace that comes with letting it go? It's a very simple question, and yet sometimes the answer is complex because holding onto anger can be strangely compelling. You will be astounded how much holding onto the anger will lose its allure once you have experienced the peace that comes from clearing it out.

SEEING ANOTHER POINT OF VIEW

One of the biggest game changers when you are angry at someone is seeing things from another point of view. We are not talking about "right vs. wrong." We are talking about trying to see things from another person's perspective—what might cause them to act the way they do.

A wonderful example of using this principle involves a traffic light near my home. Recent changes now require cars in the turning lane to stop about 30 feet before the intersection. This new change is clearly marked by a bold line indicating that cars must stop well in advance of the intersection. If a car fails to stop at this new designated line, the left turn signal never turns on and therefore causes a traffic jam.

It astonished me how many cars ignored the bold white line and I would become so frustrated as the car in front of me would prevent the left turn arrow from ever displaying on the traffic light. This caused the cars to yield to oncoming traffic instead of having a left turn arrow. Consequently, I often wasted a lot of extra time at this intersection particularly when I was in a big hurry. And then the answer suddenly dawned on me one afternoon when I was endlessly sitting at this light. And it was only after applying this new idea that I could let go and successfully clear out the anger.

I had to recognize that these people weren't doing this on purpose in an attempt to hold up traffic! They simply didn't know any better and were unaware that the road sensor was behind the bold line. They weren't consciously trying to prevent the left turn arrow from appearing. Had they known the road sensor that prompts the left turn arrow to appear was embedded behind the first bold line, they most certainly would have stopped in the right spot.

People are seldom doing things to be mean or intentionally upset you. They are usually doing the best they can based on the what they know and how much they have learned. Most people are unaware that when they harbor anger towards another person it will make them miserable and wind up coloring every aspect of their life because we have to live with the effects of the stuff that we carry. Therefore, people are often driven by anger and are powerless to clear it out.

This simple shift in my thinking did the trick, and I was able to continue with the seven steps and let go of the anger and frustration that I had been unable to release.

This trick only works when you have the DESIRE to see the other person's point of view, which is not always an easy thing to do.

When I am willing and able to see the person's point of view, I am able to completely let go. However, in those cases where I've been more interested in winning the argument, I am less likely to completely clear out all the stuff. Despite directly confronting the emotions, speaking my mind to the person to get things off my chest, and all the other steps, a kernel of anger can still remain. Even though it will significantly lighten, it will not completely clear out until I am willing to change my perspective.

When people mistreat me, I've learned to come to terms with the fact that people are often doing the best they can based on their understanding, upbringing, and what they have learned. This might be the best they can do. As in the case of the traffic light, if they knew there was a different way to behave that would have more positive results, in most cases they would avail themselves of it.

In fact, most of the time I can see that the person mistreating me is not happy. People who are mistreating you are almost always doing so from a place of anger, insecurity, resentment, or other forms of stuff. They are not acting this way from a place of wholeness, happiness, and contentment. These people have to live with the consequences of carrying around a heavy burden of stuff without any way to put it down.

It's difficult to be happy while living with so much anger and frustration. In one case, the person's behavior had actually distanced him from his entire family. Had he known his behavior had pushed away those closest to him, he surely would have done things differently. His unhappiness and struggle have had a tremendous influence on his actions and why he is mistreating others and unaware of another option.

As hard as it may sound, if we can recognize these people as fellow humans who are carrying a heavy burden, it can help us to see them through the eyes of compassion. When you see people through compassion you are seeing them through your heart rather than through your stuff. Besides, hanging onto the emotional pain hurts you just as much, if not more, than the person or life situation that triggered your stuff.

Even in situations where it is difficult to see someone through this perspective, the seven steps can clear out many layers of stuff and turn down the volume and intensity significantly. Each time another layer clears out, it will return much lighter. This is the magic ingredient that necessitates the willingness to completely let go: recognizing the other person's point of view and what has motivated their behavior.

Seeing people with your heart as a fellow traveler will usually pave the way for clearing out the stuff completely. We've already mentioned that this is part of Step 7, which is having compassion for someone. Seeing people in this manner will allow you to let go of even the last drop of resentment and return to happiness.

THE GREATEST OBSTACLE TO CLEARING OUT ANGER AND OTHER FORMS OF STUFF

A number of years ago, somebody had spread vicious rumors about a close friend of mine. The rumors were ultimately proven false; but while the situation unfolded, it was almost unbearable to watch. I had never witnessed someone mistreat a close friend or family member in this way.

As much as I tried, I just couldn't understand why someone would act so cruel and hurt a person in such a deep and profound way. My friend's life unraveled in many ways, and he was ostracized by many members of the community.

And it appeared my friend wasn't the only person this individual had hurt. A few other friends and relatives confided in me that this person had also victimized them in various ways. The list of people hurt by this individual continued to grow at a dizzying pace; it was baffling.

Having to watch my friend deal with the aftermath of this person's behavior deeply upset me. In my mind, anyone who would spread false information about someone in a way that was so hurtful and vindictive was unforgivable. In fact, I was seething with anger and hatred for this person. I couldn't stand to even look at him. I would lie awake at night wondering how anyone could mistreat someone in such a cruel manner.

Even after the rumors were proven to be false, I continued to despise this person. I couldn't summon the willingness to let go of the anger. I didn't want to let go; I wanted this person condemned for what he had done to people I care about.

At that time in my life, I had been working on clearing out layers and layers of stuff. The anger I held onto for this person seemed to diminish a lot over the years that followed, but it never quite went away. From time to time, I would run into this person and another layer of stuff would rise to the surface. It was like a never-ending cycle. Would I ever get to the bottom of the barrel and completely clear out this seemingly endless barrage of stuff?

One day after running into this person, a highly intuitive friend told me it was time to let go. She told me she sensed I was still holding onto some anger towards this person. I know she was one hundred percent correct! After hearing her words, I felt a real acknowledgement deep inside of me that I was finally ready and willing to let go of this smoldering anger.

I went home and asked from the bottom of my heart, with a deep and intense sincerity, to be free of the anger I had carried with me. I asked as sincerely as possible to have all the stuff cleared out.

After asking repeatedly I felt a tremendous change inside of me. Things shifted and I felt an exhilarating relief come over me. It honestly felt like the weight of the world had lifted off my chest. I was amazed at what I allowed myself to carry around for so long and how incredibly liberating and expansive it felt to completely let go.

This last point highlights just how important willingness is and what a pivotal role it plays in this process. If you don't have the desire and willingness to let go, it doesn't matter how many letters you write or requests you put out into the world. They will definitely have an impact but only to the extent that you are willing to let go.

Since this amazing release, I am still astounded that I no longer feel anger or hatred towards this person. It feels calm and easy, as though it was never a big deal. But it was a big deal. Only when I was willing to allow the stuff to be cleared out did the peace finally come.

A HUGE SURPRISE

After I released this anger, I was surprised at how it affected other areas of my life. The amount of anger getting triggered in other areas of my life decreased dramatically. Even in other life situations where I would normally feel a twinge of anger, I felt peace. And in situations where I would have felt a lot of anger, instead I felt very little.

It was a testament to the fact that life can only trigger what is already there. If you are carrying around a lot of anger, you will feel that same anger surface in many life situations, even though they may have little to do with one another. We will discuss this concept in more detail in the next chapter on relationships.

WHEN ALL ELSE FAILS

Because we can get swept up with anger, sometimes all the techniques go out the window! If you get angry, here is a quick check list to keep in mind.

1) **The True Source.** Remember that the only way to restore your peace is to clear out the anger rather than focusing on the person or event that triggered it and brought it to the surface. This doesn't mean that you shouldn't try to change a bad situation or address someone who is mistreating you. Just remember that nothing needs to change in order for you to be at peace other than clearing out the stuff which is standing in the way of peace.

2) Let Go for Your Sake. You don't let go of anger for the other person's sake, but for YOUR SAKE—your peace of mind depends on it. Just as it would be nuts not to heal a broken nose if someone wrongfully punched you, why would you continue to harbor anger and suffer the consequences because somebody upset you? You are much better off letting the anger go for your sake.

3) See their Point of View. Try to see the other person's point of view even if you think it's absurd. People are usually not intentionally trying to upset you. If you can see the situation through their lens, it can help you obtain a willingness to let go.

4) Have Compassion for Others. Recognize that the people are doing the best they can with the tools they have acquired. They are usually not trying to purposely annoy you. Try to have compassion for them as fellow human beings who are trying to be as happy as they can with the tools they have. If they knew a better way of doing things, they would probably try it.

Some people might have plenty of tools available to deal with their stuff, but feel burdened by and buried beneath its weight. Stuff has a way of making us unhappy, angry and bitter. This blanket of stuff can often cloud our judgement and cause us to act out in an angry and irrational manner. In many cases, the anger and discontent we harbor inside gets projected onto someone else rather than being seen at its source.

5) Summon the Willingness to Let Go. Only you know in your heart if and when you are truly ready to let go. Each moment that you carry around the stuff affords you yet another opportunity to let it go.

Each moment is a chance to ask yourself if you are willing to let go in order to be at peace or continue to carry around the backpack. The decision is always yours. Just remember that letting go is where your happiness is hiding and can restore your peace of mind whenever you are ready.

All these steps can assist you in reaching a point where you are ready and willing to completely let go of the stuff. And that's where the magic happens.

CHAPTER 6 SUMMARY

Regardless of the form it might take, you can clear stuff out. Different kinds of stuff can benefit from different approaches.

If you have been victimized, you don't have to wait for some kind of perceived "justice" in order to clear it out. You always have the choice to clear out stuff when you are ready to let go.

Dive right into your feelings and allow yourself to process the emotions using the seven steps.

Guilt serves no purpose other than the one you give it. Only you can make yourself feel guilty. Only you can decide the moment of your release.

You can clear out and transform a negative self-image by repeating positive things about yourself and clearing out the stuff that gets triggered as a result of these statements.

Even sadness, which can be quite daunting, can be cleared out like any other form of stuff.

While there are some forms of sadness and despair that are chemical (and only a licensed healthcare professional can make that determination), the techniques in this chapter can complement the therapeutic process.

Fear does not differ from any other form of stuff, regardless of how terrifying it might seem.

Working with the seven steps can release years of harbored anger.

To fully let go of anger, it can be helpful to take some additional steps outlined in this chapter.

7

A New Era of Relationships

USING THE MAGIC FOR SUCCESSFUL RELATIONSHIPS

Stuff can be the ultimate party pooper when it comes to relationships. Many of us would like to connect to our partner more deeply but our stuff is constantly getting in the way. Anger, resentment, and other forms of stuff can often dominate our relationships and sabotage our ability to connect with each other. This chapter will show you how to transform your relationships and get back to all the great things that attracted you to each other in the first place.

You will now learn the six principles to incorporate into your current relationships that build on what we've covered so far in this book. These principles expand on the seven magic steps we have been discussing and can dramatically transform relationships by breaking the endless cycle of conflict that never seems to get resolved. The principles can also show how to stop dragging stuff around and finally clear it out. This allows us to stop seeing our partner through our stuff and begin seeing this person with our heart. We are then in a much better position to use our relationships to further grow and connect—not only with our significant other but also with ourself.

Relationships are a tremendous opportunity for us to heal ourselves by releasing the stuff we have been carrying around. And few things trigger stuff as much as relationships. Within relationships, we feel fear, insecurity, anger, and everything in between—giving us an opportunity to heal. Since it's much easier to avoid confronting all of this uncomfortable stuff, we often manage to elude it for many years. Once we decide to face these patterns and clear them out, we become happier people who are much more in touch with ourselves. In turn, this allows us to connect to others in a deeper and more profound way.

The simple fact is that it's difficult to connect to anyone, including ourselves, when we have all of this stuff getting in the way. As we've already discussed, our stuff has a way of never healing and continuing to smolder in the background. Until we confront the anger and clear it out, it will keep popping up and thwarting our attempts at communicating and connecting with our partner. This chapter has a clear way out of this dilemma. Although we are focusing on romantic relationships, we can apply these principles to any relationship.

It's important to take the time to sit down with your significant other and agree to put these principles and techniques into action. By agreeing to practice them, you will take a huge step towards profoundly transforming your relationship.

THE MAGIC FORMULA FOR BETTER RELATIONSHIPS: SIX INGREDIENTS

1) Stuff is okay

First, make a pact with each other so you both have an understanding that stuff will sometimes get activated and there's nothing wrong with that. Recognize that there is no reason to judge each other because you have stuff. Everyone on the planet has stuff! We each have insecurities, anger, sadness, fear—many of which are a product of our own childhood or past relationships. They are not stupid or silly. It's just stuff we picked up along the way and never put down. In many cases, we aren't even aware that we are carrying it!

Let your significant other know that it's okay to have stuff surface. This allows your relationship to become a means to heal all the stuff you have been harboring, rather than a place to stir it up. Remember: do not judge any emotion as bad or wrong or stupid. It is just an emotion… just stuff.

2) Acknowledge the real cause of ongoing arguments

Acknowledge that many arguments aren't really about the argument itself but yesterday's stuff being stirred up again today. In other words, we often carry around stuff we've never healed, and so it keeps moving from one argument to the next. That's why we sometimes have such intense arguments about such trivial things. It's not the content of the argument that is making it so intense, but the underlying stuff that never healed. Yesterday's argument is providing the fuel for today's disagreement. Heal the stuff once and for all and end the vicious cycle.

If you don't clear out yesterday's stuff, tomorrow's intense argument about something as benign as having the television volume up too loud won't really be about the television at all. It will actually be about the underlying stuff that has crept up again because it was never cleared out. You might not even know why you are so worked up about a seemingly trivial argument. The argument is really your unhealed stuff resurfacing from a previous argument and being projected onto your significant other watching a very loud television.

By addressing the underlying stuff right away instead of continuously repackaging it into different arguments, you can nip it in the bud. There's little room for anger to build. Sure, you can still be annoyed by your significant other watching loud television, and you will certainly want to discuss it. However, it no longer needs to escalate to an intense argument. The fuel for the argument, which is the unhealed stuff from previous arguments, simply won't be there because the underlying charge has been cleared out.

Some couples have been accumulating stuff for years so even the slightest trigger can evoke an intense emotional response. You feel like you're walking on eggshells because you and your significant other are always getting angry about the small things rather than clearing them out and moving on with your life. It's astoundingly easy to get caught up in this cycle for years. Once you become aware of this cycle, you can begin to break it.

Step 2 is acknowledging the mechanics of the many arguments we have. This affords us the opportunity to look beneath the surface and avoid getting caught up in this endless cycle. In Step 2, you're asked to look a bit deeper when arguments arise. Try to determine if this anger is in response to the argument or something much deeper. If so, you can work on the underlying anger and escape this quandary.

3) Create a safe haven for expressing yourself and practicing the seven magic steps

Having a safe haven within your relationship where it's okay to express your stuff is a complete game changer. Sometimes you need to talk about your emotions and express them before you can let them go. To this end, you can create a safe haven within your relationship allowing you to express emotions within a safe environment. This is an understanding you and your significant other can have that it's okay to express your stuff for the purpose of clearing it out rather than continuously projecting it back and forth. It also gives you permission to yell and scream and stew for a little while for the express purpose of working through the stuff and letting it go.

4) The Miraculous Hour

The Miraculous Hour is one of the best things you can do for your relationship to bypass conflict. The key is to set aside some time each week (the specific amount of time is not important) to sit and talk with your partner about absolutely anything on your mind. This is essentially a "time out" from normal conversation where you drop the stuff and allow yourselves to talk about anything for these two very important reasons: expressing yourself and better understanding your partner.

The Miraculous Hour is not about forcing your opinion on your significant other. It's about expressing yourself. It's about asking any questions on your mind. It's about discussing any subject with the goal of understanding and communicating rather than arguing and being right. Try to suspend your defense mechanisms as much as possible during this time period. Allow each other to discuss any topic no matter how sensitive or trivial the topic might be. Recognize that the ultimate goal of any question is to gain greater clarity and understanding in order to improve your relationship.

Most of us have many topics that trigger our stuff and make it difficult to have a real conversation about it. For example, the topic of house hunting would always make my wife want to run. I had picked out several houses I thought were good options for us and showed them to her. I could tell she opposed my selections, but wouldn't discuss it further. Whenever I would bring up the topic, she would cut the conversation short. I wondered why she wasn't interested and would get so defensive when I would ask to talk about it. She would quickly become annoyed and change the subject. Since the conversation was off the table, I would insert little sound bites about house hunting randomly within text messages or while she was brushing her teeth. This back and forth was driving both of us crazy!

During one Miraculous Hour with my wife, I brought up the house hunting topic. Since she didn't feel threatened, we were able to have a lengthy discussion. She knew the goal was to connect and discuss whatever was on our mind without trying to argue or be combative. I could understand where she was coming from. She had the opportunity to explain herself. I was able to get things off my chest without forcing the issue or making her feel interrogated about the house.

It is vital to put away your cell phone, turn off the television, and remove any other distractions during the Miraculous Hour. Try to remove all distractions without any interruptions unless it's an emergency. The point of this exercise is to spend time away from your stuff and to connect and communicate with your significant other. This affords a tremendous opportunity to cut through the stuff and understand your partner much better.

Sometimes you will need to experience your emotions before you will be able to let them go. Acknowledge ahead of time that each of you will take responsibility for your stuff—recognizing that its source is within. If you're expressing emotion, keep in mind you're expressing it for the ultimate purpose of letting it go rather than getting one another worked up and angry.

Not having time is a poor excuse. The whole world is busy. Everyone has priorities. Make this conversation a priority and you will suddenly realize that you have time for it.

5) Stay Awake

Whenever either one of you is in the throes of emotion, agree to avoid becoming so preoccupied that you can get completely consumed with the emotions. Try to retain a small part of yourself that remembers it's just stuff and that you have the power to clear it out. As mentioned in the chapter on grief, it is possible for a small part of yourself to be aware of what is happening while experiencing powerful emotions at the same time. This part of yourself that is observing the scene can help you experience the emotion for the purpose of letting it go rather than becoming completely consumed with it.

The argument will still be the argument, but you won't be fooled by all the stuff or allow yourself to get totally lost in it. When you recognize that it's just stuff and know it is being expressed for the purpose of letting it take that course of action, you'll think twice about spewing the anger back and forth with no conclusion.

6) Take the "Bed Pledge"

Commit never to go to bed without asking to have the stuff cleared out. This entails taking time to talk about and express your emotions and then to ask that any residual stuff be cleared out by writing or asking to have it cleared out. Pledge to write a letter each night asking to clear out all of your stuff from today so it can be worked on throughout the night.

No matter what else you do, make sure you write that letter before you go to sleep! Ask yourself if you want to continue to take that burden of anger to bed with you and into the next day. Is it worth trying to sleep with all of that heaviness that can prevent you from getting a good night's sleep? Is it worth hauling around all of that anger the next day and beyond? Not only is it exhausting, but it prevents you from being present and productive. Most of all, it prevents you from feeling close to your loved ones.

Revel in the anger for an hour or two or however long it takes, but DON'T TAKE IT TO BED with you. Take the time to express it; talk about it; and experience it. Then write the letter or make the request asking to have it cleared out. This assures that you will never wake up the next day still carrying yesterday's stuff. It also assures that you will never wake up feeling the same way that you did the previous day. And finally, it assures that today's stuff won't ruin the way that you experience tomorrow.

This is something I always practice for completely selfish reasons. I don't want to go to bed taking all that heavy stuff with me! It will prevent me from sleeping well, and I will wake up feeling heavy and weighted down. I allow myself to stew for as long as necessary. However, I will always apologize and try to discuss things with my wife before bed in order to write the letter.

Even if you have not resolved the argument, you can still let go of the stuff and resolve to continue the discussion tomorrow. This allows you both to go to bed feeling much lighter and wake up feeling great.

Relationship Example

Let's look at a real-world example. Suppose your significant other completely forgets about your anniversary and makes other plans for the evening. What's normally a special occasion for you somehow gets completely forgotten this year.

An event like this not only triggers a tremendous amount of stuff, it also gives plenty of energy to the mental narrator mentioned in Chapter 1. At this point, the mental narrator goes into overdrive and tells you how inconsiderate and insensitive your partner must be.

This person obviously doesn't care about me. This person does not prioritize me. What did I do to deserve this?

If you listen to these thoughts, they will only fuel more stuff. They can create a vicious cycle where you quickly find yourself drowning in stuff! Years of stuff that never has properly healed can also come to the surface—potentially causing the situation to spiral out of control.

The Peaceful Alternative

It's important to understand that we are not trying to justify what happened. Your significant other forgot about a day that both of you consider to be quite significant and meaningful. It's completely understandable to be upset or hurt. But there are two different ways you can handle this.

The situation needs to be addressed so you can vent your feelings and get things off your chest. The big decision is if you want to do this with a focus towards clearing out the stuff rather than mindlessly staying angry and resentful. If you are arguing and yelling with no clear plan in mind, you might wind up staying in that place for a long time.

If you continue to hold onto this, chances are you won't get a good night's sleep and will continue to feel the effects the next day. It can then creep up in a number of ways and continue to wreak havoc on your relationship.

Suppose your significant other's birthday is coming up later this week. If you don't resolve this stuff, you might have unresolved anger simmering just beneath the surface. One false move could cause you to become irrationally angry, as yesterday's anger is shot right to the surface. The stuff will live on until it is given the attention that it deserves, potentially spoiling the birthday.

PUTTING IT ALL TOGETHER

Let's briefly run through the six steps outlined at the beginning of this chapter and illustrate how they would operate in this example regarding the anniversary.

1) **Acknowledge the Real Cause of Arguments.** Don't forget the true source. While it's true in this case that your partner triggered your anger, remember that the missed anniversary and the anger don't have to be forever interconnected. You can work through the steps and clear out the anger allowing you to move forward without carrying this stuff. All that is required is a decision to choose peace by focusing on releasing the stuff and utilizing the steps.

2) **Stuff is OKAY.** Therefore, it's okay to have anger, sadness, disappointment, or any other emotion that you might be feeling. Don't

deny it, suppress it, or resist it. Allow these emotions to be present without judging them as wrong or bad. It's okay to be mad as hell that you don't get to spend your anniversary with your loved one!

3) Create a Safe Haven to Express Yourself. Now that you have established a safe haven to express emotion for the purpose of letting go, it's time to express yourself! You might verbally tell your partner what you are feeling. It's okay to raise your voice and express emotion; keep in mind you are expressing your emotions for the ultimate purpose of releasing them. Make sure you establish this goal when you are not embroiled in an argument and things are relatively calm. Within this context, you can explain how angry it makes you feel that your anniversary will be spent alone. It's okay to vent and speak your mind in order to let the anger go.

4) The Miraculous Hour. This is obviously a great time to get everything off your chest which is why this time is so important. Always make sure that your intention is to let this anger go rather than continue to carry it with you.

5) Stay Awake. While you are experiencing the emotions, remember to have at least some small part of yourself observe the emotions to avoid becoming completely swept up in them. Do not mistake these emotions as yourself. See these emotions as stuff that you now have the opportunity to heal. Once they are successfully healed, they can no longer create chaos in the future.

6) Take the Bed Pledge. This would first involve deciding to let go of the stuff before going to sleep. Next, write a heartfelt letter or make a sincere request to have the stuff cleared out before you go to sleep. Ask from the heart to have all the stuff cleared out while you sleep and be prepared to repeat this process over the next few days.

Remember to do this ONLY after you feel you are ready to let go. You will probably need time to express your emotions and talk about them before you are ready to clear it out. When you feel you are ready, ask as sincerely as you can to have the stuff completely cleared out. Then let go and forget about it. The rest of the work will be done for you, and you will lighten up in one of the ways described in Chapter 4.

You are not doing this for your partner. This is ultimately for your own peace of mind. Clearing out the stuff will make you so much happier and allow you to peacefully enjoy the evening. You choose to use the magic steps for your own sake, so you can return to underlying happiness. Happiness is always the natural result of letting go of stuff.

These six steps are a game changer for your relationships and can completely transform them. It's a new way to live that allows everybody to travel much lighter and happier.

CHAPTER 7 SUMMARY

Stuff can seriously interfere with your relationship with your partner.

As you clear out stuff, you will be able to see your partner through your heart and connect more directly.

Arguments and discord are often the same old stuff being recycled and spewed back and forth. It might look like a new argument each time, but it's the old stuff getting stirred up and repackaged from a previous argument. Unresolved emotion keeps refueling different arguments.

It's okay to have stuff—everybody has stuff!

Set aside time each day to talk to your partner for the purpose of expressing yourself and be better understood. Designate this time as a "safe space" where it is okay to express emotion in order to release it. During this time, it is possible to set aside your stuff and discuss things in a less confrontational way.

Try to stay alert whenever you experience emotions so the stuff doesn't overtake you. Experience the emotion for the ultimate purpose of letting go.

Never go to bed without asking to have any active stuff cleared out.

Try to speak to your partner and process emotions before you go to bed. This allows you to process stuff while you sleep so you wake up feeling much clearer in the morning.

8

All Things Esoteric

This last section is not for everybody. If you are a "just the facts" kind-of-person, you can successfully work with the techniques in this book with much success. You do not have to believe in or work with anything that you consider mystical or strange. However, if you are interested in things that might seem outside-the-box, then this section has your name on it!

LEARNING TO SENSE THE STUFF

It may come as a surprise that stuff is actually energy and can therefore be sensed on a number of levels and in a variety of ways. Many of us have already had this experience in one way or another. Have you ever shopped around for a house and when walking into it, you felt instantly repulsed by the energy of the house? Perhaps the house had some kind of negative feeling which is residual stuff from past residents. Or maybe you felt tense and uneasy. Whether it's a house, a car, or a person, this energy we feel is residual stuff. This stuff can continue to hang around in a variety of different ways and locations. Maybe some people make you feel uneasy whenever you see them or even think about them. Even the mere mention of their names makes your skin crawl.

Have you ever had someone say, "I love you" but the delivery left you feeling disappointed because it sounded flat and lifeless? While saying "I love you" would usually evoke a positive response, if the words lack emotion and power, it will usually wind up feeling dull and disingenuous. What really gives the words oomph is when they are uttered sincerely and from the heart—with intention and energy.

A hug works the same way. Some hugs can feel completely empty while other times the warmth is palpable.

Written words can be sensed as well. Someone can write you a letter that feels alive and sincere while another letter might feel devoid of any real emotion as though it was mindlessly written.

We can sense and feel other people's stuff. We can feel fear, anger, and sadness because they have definitive energetic signatures. Though we are swimming in a sea of energy, many of us have tuned it out in favor of our thoughts and physical senses.

Notice all the stuff around you, including your own stuff. The next time you walk into a room or enter someone else's car try to become more aware of the stuff around you and what you are feeling. Pay attention to how different the energies feel. I assure you that every single form of stuff has a very distinct feeling.

Someone under a tremendous amount of emotional duress will have a very distinct energetic signature. On the other hand, anger simply feels angry, and you will actually be able to sense it in your heart area. Sadness and depression look and feel dark, heavy, and sad. Someone who is happy has a distinctive lighter and open energy.

When you meet a person or think about a person you know, you can ask yourself the following questions:

Do I feel any kind of stuff associated with these people?

Does the stuff feel dense and heavy or light and happy?

Does the stuff feel angry? If so, how angry? Is it mild irritation or full-on rage?

Does the energy feel sexual?

Does the energy feel chemical in nature, such as recreational or prescription drugs?

Each form of energy or stuff has a distinctive energetic signature and, as such, will feel a certain way. You can learn to correlate these feelings to the specific form of stuff.

We could discuss this in much greater detail, but the point is simple. Everything is energy and therefore, emits a specific frequency that can be felt and sensed. We all have a natural, innate ability to pick up on this energy. You can begin to notice how different people feel when you are around them or even when you think about them. By becoming aware of the different nuances that each form of stuff has associated with it, you can begin to correlate with each energy. This will allow you to become more in touch with other people and yourself.

Learning how to develop and refine this ability is quite possible. And though we do not dive deeper into the topic for this reading, you can learn more about this work through my online and in-person seminars in the back of this book.

Yes, stuff can be sensed in a variety of ways. It's important to keep in mind that no matter how it feels, all stuff is energy and energy can be cleared out. It never has to become a permanent part of your identity.

Here are some exercises you can do to learn how to sense stuff:

Exercise #1. Select two different people you know and try to focus on each one individually. Notice how each one looks and feels. Can you sense any differences between the two? Perhaps one has a heavier and darker energy than the other. One might look more weighted down emotionally or by medication. Does one feel angrier than the other? Focus on their name and how it feels to be around them. It's astounding how much information you can pick up through this process.

Exercise #2. Now, have a friend select two people whom you have never met and have them give you their first names only. Follow the same process as above and pay attention to the kinds of information you elicit. Try tuning in to each person's energy and see what kinds of information you can receive. Does the first person seem lighter than the second, or vice versa? Does one seem brighter than the other? Perhaps one has a higher energy than the other or one might look and feel sad. You might be astounded at the results of these exercises and how much information you have been routinely filtering out from your awareness.

STUFF, ENERGY, AND KARMA

Another consequence of stuff being energy is that it attracts other energy of a like frequency and vibration. When you fail to release stuff and continue to hold onto it, it will attract particular kinds of people and situations into your life in order to activate the stuff and force you to confront it.

At this point, you are faced with a choice. You can either heal the pattern by clearing it out or allow it to go dormant. If it goes dormant, life will throw other people and circumstances at you to make you more conscious of this pattern until you confront it.

For example, if you are harboring anger you have not yet faced, you will often encounter people and life circumstances that trigger this anger and make it more conscious. Before it was triggered, the pattern might have been largely unconscious and unrecognized. Now that it has come to the surface, you are forced to confront it and heal it. Otherwise, you will become angry for a certain period of time until it goes dormant again.

Another example is a friend who had a constant fear of germs. It never surprised me when he would complain about how he was seated next to people who wouldn't stop coughing! Since these energies and emotions—anger, fear, and sadness—each has its own unique frequency and energetic signature, they will automatically attract like things to you.

The very things that we hide inside and avoid confronting are the driving force behind the people and events that come into our lives for the very purpose of bringing these things to light. When the stuff surfaces, we are confronted by those energies and are forced to face them. This provides us with the opportunity to heal the anger, pain, fear, sadness, guilt, grief, etc.

Life provides us with opportunities to heal the things we need to work on the most by activating our stuff.

Now that these patterns are active, we are faced with a choice. We can go about our business and continue with the status quo by harboring these energies in a never-ending process of having the stuff come up and then going dormant every time we avoid dealing with it. Or we can choose to become conscious about the process by starting to heal these energies and clear out this stuff once and for all.

Until we come to terms with our stuff and heal it, it will continuously resurface under different guises and events. Keep in mind, the underlying energy that gets triggered is the same energy that keeps surfacing and resurfacing. This is karma.

Karma is nothing more than the consequence of holding onto old emotional patterns we refer to as stuff. This causes us to react to people and situations in a very distinct way. If you are harboring lots of anger, often even the minor things will trigger this anger and present a tremendous challenge when dealing with certain people.

Until these energies or stuff heal, you will continue to carry around this karma. If you don't heal it and let it go, you will continuously face these kinds of people and circumstances that arise in response to this energy. To get rid of the pattern, you must decide to face the underlying emotions or stuff that you have been hiding from all of this time.

Ultimately, there is nowhere to hide. Wherever you go, your stuff is right there with you. If you are harboring pain and sadness, you might take a vacation, get a new job, or even move to another country. All these things are diversionary tactics designed to distract you from the true underlying root cause of your sadness, anger, fear, or other forms of stuff. And none of these tactics will work. The only surefire way to heal your pain is to come face to face with it and clear it out.

The solution is seeing these emotions that surface as just stuff that can be cleared out rather than becoming completely identified and consumed with these emotions—amplifying them to create even more stuff. If you don't recognize the stuff as stuff, you will allow the emotion, such as anger, to engulf you. In this case, the person consumed with anger is generating more anger that will either go dormant until it is triggered another day or become part of this person's daily background. More and more anger will start coloring their experience. The same is true for sadness, guilt, fear, and other kinds of stuff we have been addressing.

Every time a person or event triggers your stuff and brings it to the surface, you are presented with a grand opportunity to release the old patterns stored in your body and energy. Only this time we can let it go instead of continuing to harbor it inside.

We don't have to keep repeating the same behavior and waging the same arguments with the same people year in and year out. A large part of what is driving us to repeat this behavior is that we have all of this unconscious stuff that keeps surfacing and we are unaware of it. We often don't realize that when the stuff comes up, it completely takes over which causes us to identify with the anger, sadness, fear, etc. We become the stuff, and the stuff becomes us. But now that we know what is really happening, we can choose to work with the stuff and break the cycle once and for all!

Every time you become aware of your stuff, it marks a pivotal moment in your evolution. Your life need not be dictated by a bunch of old emotional wiring. You can rewire your circuitry. Instead of being driven by a bunch of out-of-date stuff that has largely remained unconscious, we can begin taking steps to regain control and take back what is ours.

This is what mystics call the "unobserved mind." Simply put, this is all of our unconscious stuff that keeps surfacing and then going dormant again while we remain unaware this is happening. And, while we might be unaware of it, it controls and dictates much of our behavior operating within the backdrop of our life. We can learn to transmute this unobserved mind by becoming aware of it and utilizing the different techniques and strategies we have been discussing. We no longer have to be at the mercy of our stuff. We no longer have to listen to whatever background music happens to be playing.

This ends the cycle of repeating the same old arguments or walking around sad, fearful, or grief-stricken. Now that you know where the true source lies, you can use this as an opportunity to look your stuff right in the eye, perhaps for the very first time. Begin to work with your stuff using the seven magic steps, and you will peel away layer after layer of stuff and remove the karma. You can change the music whenever you are ready.

MANY PATHS LEAD TO THE SAME PLACE

The techniques in this book are a wonderful and effective way to clear out all your stuff and free yourself of the pain. However, there are numerous other methods and techniques that work towards this end. They can range from therapy and counseling to more esoteric healing such as energy work, meditation, visualization and hypnosis. They all are geared toward two things: 1) releasing the old emotional patterns stored within us—our stuff, and 2) reconnecting us with our true self. And each method is designed to accomplish the clearing in different ways.

For example, meditation can temporarily quiet your mind and your stuff allowing you to access the joy of connecting with your true self. Some forms of meditation will allow you to observe your mind and your emotions and will help you let go.

Some people find that running outside or being in nature helps them connect to this place. Therapy can allow you to talk about your emotions and gain insights which can often be a catalyst for moments where you spontaneously let go and release. This is where an insight into something allows you to process an emotion and release it. You will feel lighter and more at peace.

Sometimes therapy triggers emotions we've locked away in the room we discussed in Step 4 and propels our stuff to the surface.

This gives us an opportunity to examine what we've hidden in that locked room.

Massage, energy work, Network, Reiki, meditation, and different types of body work can also induce an emotional release by triggering our stuff and bringing it to the surface. Sometimes people will have an emotional release when they are undergoing various kinds of intense massage work.

MY TECHNIQUE

I work with clients using my own technique which works directly with their energy to clear things out quickly. This technique can also clear out difficult and long-standing patterns.

My technique is highly intuitive and uses a variety of ways to clear out emotional energy. The end goal is clearing out the stuff—the false self we have created—and revealing the underlying happiness hiding just beneath.

ENERGY WORK

Since stuff is a form of energy, there are various ways to work with it using techniques that manipulate the body's energy. This can be a powerful way to shift stored up emotions in the body. These techniques can be used separately or in combination with the clearing techniques in this book to enhance the process.

There are a variety of formal techniques that utilize energy work. A massage can allow us to release and clear out pent-up emotions. Reiki is a formalized system of energy work designed to facilitate energetic changes in the body which sometimes clear out stuff. There are numerous other techniques from meditation to chakra balancing. The goal is to release and let go of the stuff thereby allowing ourselves to become more connected to our source.

There are many paths that help guide us back to the same place - our true self. As I have repeatedly said throughout this book, our true self with its accompanying peace and joy, has never left us. It was simply obscured waiting to be uncovered. You need only clear it out to uncover and reveal the deep peace and joy that lies underneath.

LISTENING AND HELPING THE STUFF CLEAR

As you continue to work with the magic steps, you will become more aware of the changes that take place as stuff clears. In fact, earlier in the book, I mentioned that it's important to be aware of these changes once we have asked to have the stuff cleared out.

Some examples include feeling as though a ton of bricks have been lifted off. Or you might begin to feel lighter in a specific part of your body like the chest or stomach area. You might even feel like taking some deep breaths as you become aware that you are feeling relaxed.

In addition, when stuff begins to clear out, you might experience some intuitive urges to breathe or move in a certain way. All these are designed to aid in shifting the emotional energy and to help it clear out. It can, therefore, be very helpful to act on these urges. Listen to your body and inner wisdom and move and breathe accordingly. You might feel the urge to move your arms, take a deep breath, or place your hands on a certain part of your body. Just do whatever comes naturally. There is no right or wrong way to move or breathe. It's perfectly okay if you experience no desire to move or breathe differently. The stuff will clear out either way. As you continue to practice the magic steps and become more familiar with this work, you might begin having these subtle messages to move or breathe in a certain way, which can help the stuff clear out even more effectively.

Suppose you are feeling a sadness within your heart area and after working with the seven magic steps you feel that you are ready to let it go. While you are writing a letter or immediately afterwards you might begin to notice that your breathing has increased, and you may begin to feel the stuff getting lighter.

As the stuff clears out, you may feel prompted to place your hand over an area of your body while you allow any feelings to process. This type of energy work is highly intuitive. Trust the intuitive part of yourself to direct you where and how to place your hands. The more you practice, the easier it becomes. It can be as simple as feeling an urge to place one hand on the top of your head and another on your heart area and immediately feel the emotion beginning to shift. You might even visualize energy clearing out.

There is no correct way to do it, but I assure you that the more you practice it, the more proficient you will become. The more you notice your energy, the more you will feel moved to do things to help it lighten up. The more you allow yourself to trust these feelings, the more proficient you will become in helping the stuff to clear out.

Again, these things are not necessary for clearing out emotional stuff. All that's required: using the magic steps while making the requests to have the stuff cleared out. The energy work we are discussing here is additional information to be used in whatever way feels appropriate to you. When the energy begins shifting, these are things we can do to aid the clearing process.

WHY THIS GAME CHANGING WORK SPEEDS UP YOUR HEALING

All healing happens in an instant. You might spend years in therapy talking about your situation to reach that one moment when you achieve the understanding and desire to let go of your hurt and pain.

Each therapy session offers you the opportunity to have these moments of clarity to let go and breathe a little deeper as you talk about your feelings and achieve new insights. Progress occurs each time you gain any insight that allows you to spontaneously release stuff such as anger, guilt, and fear.

Perhaps you have been talking about your grief with a friend or counselor for several months. Suddenly you feel something shift inside you as you experience a breakthrough and the grief begins to lighten up. This breakthrough is accompanied by breathing deeper and feeling as though a weight has been lifted off your shoulders. All of this talking and analyzing affords you numerous opportunities to have insightful moments to let go of some underlying stuff you are carrying.

However, understanding your stuff is NOT always a prerequisite to letting it go. Understanding is often necessary in order for us to achieve the willingness to let it go. Sometimes we must first gain these insights through talking and therapy in order to reach a better understanding, which permits us to let go.

The truth of the matter:

You have the ability to let go in any instant.

This is what the seven magic steps are all about. Rather than passively waiting for healing to come to you or haphazardly talking about your stuff and waiting to have a breakthrough, you can now dramatically speed up the healing process by taking control of it. It can all happen at an accelerated pace, if you so desire, by taking a more active role in your healing process.

Whether you are in therapy or using another form of treatment to help you through emotional pain, the magic steps can augment this treatment by enabling you to heal much faster using these techniques to directly process and clear out the stuff. This work allows you to take the "bull by the horns" and work directly with your stuff almost immediately.

Once you recognize and experience that stuff can be cleared out and released, your desire to let go will increase dramatically. You will no longer have to talk about your stuff for many years in order to have it released a little at a time. You can accelerate the process either on its own or in a therapy session by consciously allowing the emotion to surface, talk about it, experience it with compassion, and obtain the willingness to ask for it to clear out.

And the instant you have the desire and readiness to let go, you can successfully write a letter and then get out of the way. This makes way for the magic to move in and clear out the stuff. You might start feeling lighter. Perhaps it will process while you sleep, and you will wake up feeling much happier. Healing can occur in a specific instant—the instant you decide to let go, ask for the stuff to clear out, and experience the relief.

Now you know firsthand that stuff can be cleared out at a time of your own choosing, and this will be a game changer. This will speed up your desire to let it go sooner rather than later. And when you are ready, the magic steps can work wonders. It's astounding how quickly you can obtain the willingness to let go of these emotions once you have recognized you can do it in an instant—when you choose. You are no longer at the mercy of your stuff.

THIS IS NOT A RACE

You don't have to be in a hurry to rush this process along. Be at peace with whatever comes up on any given day and work through the steps. This is not a race. The goal is not to move through the stuff as quickly as possible before you are even ready to let go. Remember to allow the process to unfold. You will clear out what you need each day. You cannot rush this journey if your heart is not in it.

Once you see that stuff can be cleared out, you will quickly learn that it doesn't have to be carried around any longer than necessary. In fact, you will see how quickly you can process and move through it. The most important ingredient you can have is the willingness to confront your stuff and then let it go. The more you practice this work and the more results you see, the more your willingness will grow. You will therefore require less time before you are ready to clear out the stuff. And since your desire will be so much stronger, you will begin working with the seven magic steps almost immediately after stuff arises.

STUFF AND YOUR HEALTH

Holding onto stuff is not good for your health. The connection between emotional stress and physical ailments have been well documented for quite some time.

Just a modicum of research on the internet will reveal a plethora of peer-reviewed research papers documenting the effects of stress, grief, anxiety, and other emotions on the body and overall wellbeing. Countless studies have warned about the effects of stress, anxiety, anger, and grief on blood pressure, heart health, and hormone levels.

And this is just the tip of the iceberg as we have only recently learned the effects of stuff on our overall health and well-being. And the evidence continues to mount. This book is not meant to be an exhaustive list of research. My only intent is to awaken your curiosity and interest on the subject prompting you to conduct your own research on this topic.

I believe, wholeheartedly, that our health is affected by stuff in more ways than we can imagine. Remember that stuff is energy and has a particular energetic signature. I believe that when we continue to hold onto these energy patterns, they begin to affect our health. The particular vibrations of these frequencies can be harmful to our health long term as they begin to manifest physically. This can alert us that we need to start listening and becoming more in touch with ourselves.

We are only beginning to understand the mind-body connection and still know nothing about the mechanism of consciousness. It seems clear that our emotions can have a powerful effect on our health, and we will no doubt continue to study this for many years to come.

Perhaps as we learn even more about the connection between our emotions, mind, and physical health, it will become an even bigger part of the overall clinical picture. The medical community will hopefully continue to become more concerned about our emotional health as it relates to our physical health and will uncover even more relationships between the two.

THE PHASES OF THIS WORK PHASE 1: CLEARING OUT THE PAST

Phase 1 is what we have been discussing so far throughout this book.

This phase is a giant leap forward where you can utilize the magic steps to clear out stuff AFTER it has already become active. In many cases, the stuff has already been wreaking havoc on you and now you are ready to clear it out and let it go. It's a wonderful achievement and can dramatically change your life.

Whenever something triggers your stuff, be cognizant of what decision you are making. Are you going to get caught up in the stuff and become angry, sad, or scared? Or do you choose to work with the magic and restore peace?

PHASE 2: THE NEXT LEVEL OF MASTERY

Becoming more conscious of this process is the next phase of mastery in this work.

Suppose someone makes you extremely angry. Even while you are experiencing the anger that is getting triggered, it is possible for you to simultaneously use the magic. You can observe it and allow it to fully surface, and immediately express a clear desire to let it go. Instead of getting angry and then trying to work with the magic, you can begin practicing it right there on the spot. The key is to involve something I like to call "The Golden Moment."

The Golden Moment

One key to begin working on the stuff immediately instead of allowing the stuff to overtake us is the "Golden Moment."

When we go through painful situations or when someone angers us, there will be a specific moment that gives us the opportunity to decide how we wish to proceed. We can either let the stuff overtake us or we can begin to consciously work with it by utilizing the seven magic steps immediately. This golden moment holds the key to how we will process the stuff.

Suppose someone angers you. A moment exists when you can decide whether you want to hang onto the anger or let it go. We often make these decisions without paying any attention to them. In a split second, we might decide to hold onto the anger and allow it to consume us and overtake us. For many people, this has become a process they hardly notice any more.

In a split second, we can make a conscious decision to work through those magical steps that will help us let go. We can immediately remind ourself that we are not the stuff and we can experience it for the sole purpose of letting go rather than identifying with it and becoming overwhelmed with anger.

Initially, this might only work for something we are willing to release almost immediately. There will still be plenty of situations where we will need to work through things one layer at a time by gradually working through the magic steps. But there are people who have completely mastered this technique and can clear out virtually any form of stuff almost immediately while it is still happening! This is definitely something to strive for as it is obtainable.

The more often you practice clearing out stuff, the less tolerance you will have for stuff and the stronger your willingness will become to let it go immediately. You will surprise yourself at how much faster you are willing to let go and to ask for the stuff to clear out. Holding onto stuff will seem much less desirable.

Who wants to be in prison a moment longer than necessary? Once you have found a way out and a doorway that leads to happiness, why would you wish to linger even a moment longer than necessary?

CLEARING OUT STUFF CAN HEAL THE WORLD

Conflict is the outward manifestation of the inner turmoil and hatred felt within each of us – the many forms of stuff that we have been discussing.

War, racism, and terrorism are all the result of what happens when different forms of stuff such as anger, hatred, and jealousy acquire a specific trigger and target. For example, racism is where a particular group of people act as a trigger for your stuff and therefore become the outward focus or "target" of all of this unhealed emotion.

Rather than seeing this particular group of people as a trigger for all of the stuff that you have been harboring such as anger, hatred, and jealousy, they are seen as the cause, and therefore, all of the stuff is directed at them.

The true way to peace is to change one heart at a time, clearing out the anger, hatred, sadness and fear within each heart. This returns each person to peace because in the absence of "stuff," peace is felt.

Once enough people have healed the stuff "within" there will be no more conflict "without."

This is one of our primary missions in life: to change darkness into light.

We are peeling the onion and removing layer after layer of the illusion of who we thought we were. We thought we were the stuff, but just underneath lies our true self. We thought we were the grief, sadness, fear, and guilt, but just underneath lies real happiness which is our true essence.

Our task is to recognize the darkness and to let it go. It is not who we are, and only our belief in it has kept this darkness in place.

All it takes to initiate tremendous healing is a decision to open the door to the stuff and begin utilizing the magic of these seven steps.
This will always lead you back to your true home in the sunlight.

AFTER THE BACKPACK

What happens after you remove the backpack?

As you begin to remove the backpack and work with the techniques in this book, you will feel lighter and more connected with your true self. You will also become keenly aware of a kind of inner voice. This voice has always been there but wasn't easily discernable amidst the clamor of all your stuff.

After the backpack has been removed, what remains is a completely new world with new sights and sounds. It is your true self. Your emotions and mind will become quieter and your soul's inner voice can be heard. These are intuitive feelings which are the sound of our souls

How do we access this voice and what it is saying? How can you utilize this wise voice in your own life?

A whole new world awaits you…

To be continued in upcoming seminars and in future books…

CHAPTER 8 SUMMARY

Stuff is energy. Therefore, it puts out a specific frequency we can sense.

As stuff clears, it is helpful to listen to any intuitive urges to aid in the clearing process.

There are many healing techniques with the same aim: to reconnect us with our natural state of happiness and wellbeing.

Stuff can impact our health.

Healing occurs in an instant. That instant can be accessed much more rapidly by practicing this work.

These steps allow you to work more consciously with your stuff and enables you to heal faster.

Your stuff will continue to attract people and situations into your life that will activate it giving you the opportunity to heal it.

Clearing out stuff can heal the world and transform inner conflict into light.

As inner conflict gets cleared out, outward conflict ceases.

Acknowledgements

To my editor, Berni Xiong, for tirelessly editing this book and catering to my seemingly endless requests—always with a smile.

To my loving and supportive wife Amy for her love, support, and encouragement.

To my sister Hallie; brother-in-law David; nephew Doni; and nieces Devorah and Dassie for their constant inspiration and encouragement to complete *Pure Emotional Magic* so they could read it and try the techniques!

To my mother Gail for her special friendship, advice, support AND for always being the most incredible Mom in the universe.

To the teachers who have inspired me to keep striving towards personal growth.

To the many people who have benefited from this work and encouraged me to write this book.

Conclusion

Congratulations! You have traveled many miles from where you started. Hopefully, you have been thinking of your emotions as something that is not permanent and can be changed whenever you are ready. Perhaps you no longer fear your emotions and recognize they cannot hurt you. And, most importantly, I hope you have had at least one experience where your emotions have either lightened up or completely cleared out. These are major accomplishments and truly call for a celebration!

PRACTICE THE TECHNIQUES

It is perfectly normal at this point to feel unsure of yourself. The good news is you don't need to have it all figured out! All this book asks of you is to practice the techniques and to trust the process.

If you are working through longstanding emotional patterns, be patient. Allow yourself to move at your own pace. Trust that the journey will bring you to the underlying peace you seek. Remember you don't have to know exactly *how* it all works. What's important is having the willingness and sustained effort to practice this work coupled with a sincere desire for change.

Please be easy on yourself. Don't try to force anything to happen or judge yourself harshly for not moving at a faster pace. Spend time each day practicing these techniques even when turbulent emotions inevitably arise. It's especially in the tough times that the techniques in this book can come in handy. Use Pure Emotional Magic as your daily guide.

TRUST THE PROCESS

As you continue to work with the steps outlined in this book, you will become more comfortable working with your emotions, and the results will begin to increase. In turn, the more success you have with these techniques, the more your confidence will grow.

As you weave these practices into your daily life, you will begin to notice changes. For some, the changes might be subtle at first—unfolding in a very gradual way. It might suddenly dawn on you that you feel lighter or more at peace about a particular issue. Others might experience more dramatic changes or manifest sweeping changes rather quickly. Regardless of your experience, the key is to get in the habit of practicing this work. The rest will take care of itself.

As you practice this work, you might feel on top of the world some days. Whatever stuff you are working on might instantly vanish leaving you with tremendous joy and happiness. At other times, it can be a bit more challenging and the stuff may need to be cleared out gradually in layers. Do not get discouraged! Even if it feels as though nothing is happening, I assure you changes are always taking place beneath the surface. The effects aren't always instantaneous.

In some cases, you won't be ready to let go. That's perfectly okay! Be patient with yourself while you practice the techniques. Clearing the stuff is not a race to the finish line. It's about being gentle with yourself and allowing the process to unfold. Forcing something to clear only strengthens its hold.

Never let your stuff fool you. Whether you are dealing with grief, loss, anger, injustice, fear or self-doubt, the magic steps are equipped to handle whatever form your stuff might take—yes, even if you might feel emotionally constipated.

Remember: Practice this work and stick with the program. Allow yourself to experience the shifts. Be ready for great changes on the horizon. And if you run into any problems, you can always contact me at joey@pureemotionalmagic.com.

I wish you much success as you journey back to the light.

About the Author

About 25 years ago, Dr. Joey Raab had a life-changing experience when he witnessed deep emotional pain miraculously vanish, leaving happiness in its wake. Since that day, his life's passion has been to learn more about what he experienced by exploring personal growth and techniques for personal healing. The burning question that became the catalyst for his work: can this healing be replicated and used by anyone to dissipate emotional pain and uncover the happiness hiding underneath?

That was the start of an amazing journey which led to a Doctor of Chiropractic degree and certification as a Reiki Master. Dr. Raab continued his passion by delving into more healing education including Kriya Yoga, Network Chiropractic, Pre-cognitive Re-education, and *A Course in Miracles*.

As Dr. Raab's intuitive abilities have grown, he has developed his own techniques for emotional clearing and healing. He combines his strong intuitive abilities with years of practicing energetic and emotional healing when working with clients. He also teaches Pure Emotional Magic (PEM), a healing technique he created which is the title of this book. The PEM approach enables clients to clear out their "emotional backpacks" and rediscover the underlying peace and joy.

It is Dr. Raab's hope that by following his step-by-step instructions in this book, YOU will find and rediscover true happiness hiding "just beneath the surface."

***

For more information or to contact Dr. Joey Raab, visit pureemotionalmagic.com.

To leave an honest review and star rating, go to the book's listing on Amazon.com.

Made in United States
North Haven, CT
19 April 2022

18369645R00098